AF283975

In Quest of Beauty

Surviving Ashes and Storm

DR LYNDA INCE-GREENAWAY

THE CHOIR PRESS

Copyright © 2025 Dr. Lynda Ince-Greenaway

All rights reserved. No part of this publication may be reproduced or transmitted in any form or by any means, electronic or mechanical including photocopying, recording or any information storage or retrieval system, without prior permission in writing from the publishers.

The right of Dr. Lynda Ince-Greenaway to be identified as the author of this work has been asserted by her in accordance with the Copyright, Designs and Patents act 1988

First published in the United Kingdom in 2025 by
The Choir Press

ISBN 978-1-78963-507-2

Contents

Acknowledgements

I dedicate this book to all the brave women the world over who through their suffering become beacons of light and service to others. May God bless you.

I am indebted to God for giving me the time, energy and endurance to write this book. I confess that at times even though it was difficult to listen to the stories I heard, I am nevertheless grateful that I was given the opportunity to do this important work and bring it out into the open. Having developed my listening skills, I believe that it is a gift God has given me, so that I could go beyond merely hearing to empathic listening.

I would like to express my heartfelt thanks to the ten women who contributed to this book. It was a pleasure to share in their moments of sadness but also their moments of joy. I was given insight into their world and from that position I was able to understand what it meant for them to go through the ashes and storm and yet emerge as people with a beautiful story.

In bringing the stories together, I can look back and say that it was a project I enjoyed and that I value the opportunity to be part of other people's lives.

My sincere thanks to Dr Gozil Oxley who read and commented on the first draft of my manuscript.

Foreword

Dr Lynda Ince-Greenaway, one of my siblings, has given me the honour of writing this foreword. I have had the privilege of reading and editing the draft version of her manuscript "In Quest of Beauty."

Author of "Hard Truth: Growing out of Adversity" Dr Lynda Ince-Greenaway now provides us with another inspiring masterpiece, based on the lives of ten women who have transformed their lives from ashes to beauty.

The themes and lessons in this book are not only timely but timeless. Dr Lynda Ince-Greenaway uses her skill and experience as a professional social worker, mentor and life coach. Through reflective analysis she extrapolates the deeper meaning from the lives of those who have faced mental, physical, and emotional tragedies, and how they have triumphed. Dr Lynda Ince-Greenaway describes these experiences in an empathic and soulful way, as she shares her own experiences of ashes that yielded positive outcomes.

"In Quest of Beauty" offers analogies of fire and storm in a way that will resonate with readers, beautifully portraying real-life stories and interpreting their meanings and solutions. The spiritual content contained in her latest book offers the reader encouragement and hope in the midst of hopelessness. The themes will attract all those who are seeking to embark on a fulfilling journey of self-discovery and will become a valuable resource.

"In Quest of Beauty" is a must-read for anyone seeking to learn from others about their transformative life-changing experiences. As you begin to read each chapter, I encourage you to do so with an open mind and heart. I'm confident that you will come away with new perspectives and a deeper understanding of your own quest for beauty.

Pauline Oxley
Author

Author's Note

I was baptised when I was twelve years old, and it felt really exciting to give my heart to the Lord. I was one among many children who made this momentous decision during their youthful days, but I have never turned back or doubted that I was a born-again Christian. I have had many challenges during my lifetime, and it was during these times that I turned to God for the answer to my trials and the testing of my faith. I always wanted to share my faith with others. As a child, I would walk the streets giving out Christian literature and urging people to come to church. I would even admonish my father to change his ways because he did not follow the path of faith. He thought that I was an upstart and impudent child. I dare say that as a child I did not have a full and complete understanding of my actions, but I knew that there was something inside of me that brought awareness of how I had to tell others about my beliefs. I was most fortunate to be raised in a family where my mother was a devout Christian and her life was like a lighthouse, always guiding me to a safe harbour. In later years I suffered considerable loss, but I was determined that adversity would not cause me to abandon my faith.

As a Christian woman I bring a Christian perspective to this book. I will be using scriptures and stories from the Bible as well my own stories and the stories of brave women that made this book possible.

My underpinning Christian values led me to consider the wisdom and guidance given in the Bible, some of it coming from the experiences of women; even though in their day women were conceived of as second-class citizens they nevertheless had influence that was often ignored or undermined. We can learn from their stories and how they responded to adversity. The narrative of Esther is inspiring as we read of how she dedicated herself to service and risked her life to save her people. She rose from being an orphan to becoming a Queen in the Persian Empire with considerable influence (Esther chapters 1–10). Equally, there is the inspiring story of

Abigail (1 Samuel:25) who despite the treatment she received from her husband became a woman of wisdom and beauty. Jesus told a parable of an unjust judge which is recorded in Luke 18:1-8. It demonstrated the determination of a widow who went to an unjust judge seeking reparation for debts due to her husband after his death. The widow had nothing and needed the money to survive. However, the unjust judge refused to dispense justice, but she persevered in presenting her case to him until he had no other choice but to do what was just and fair.

All Bible texts are taken from the King James Version.

Introduction

When our days become dreary with low-hovering clouds of despair, and when our nights become darker than a thousand midnights, let us remember that there is a creative force in this universe, working to pull down the gigantic mountains of evil, a power that is able to make a way out of no way and transform dark yesterdays into bright tomorrows.

DR MARTIN LUTHER KING JNR.

From the most affluent and celebrated people to those without notoriety, from the famous to the infamous, from the rich to the poor, from the person living in a palace to the homeless person huddled under the arches or in shop doorways, from those living in luxury to those living in impoverished communities, we are all God's children. We came from dust and ashes and we return there, whether after a straight or narrow path. The reality is that we all have one fate but, on our journey, we can take different routes, some to success and some to failure. We have the opportunity to rise like the mythical Phoenix and exchange ashes for beauty against the crucible of an experience. The characters that we develop, whether we are gifted with a short or long life span, are the legacy we leave behind. It is not the trials we endure that people remember, but how we responded to them.

When I first started to think of how and when I would retire, my first question was, what would I lose? An income was at the top of my list, but equally important was missing the routine of waking up with a specific purpose. At the forefront of my mind was that I would miss interacting with my colleagues and people I had come to know as part of my work-life. I thought that it would mean losing an aspect of my life that was fundamental to the way I functioned. There was no doubt that I had great difficulty in making the leap and thinking about the changes that would be a threat to my wellbeing. I was concerned about losing my identity as a member of the workforce. I knew that planning for this momentous event would be an important aspect of the change I would encounter. I did not want to feel that my days of usefulness would come to an end. Being active meant continuing to work, it meant being valued for my ideas and making a positive contribution to the lives of others. I saw the end of my working days as part of my struggle but as I was fast approaching the age of seventy, I knew that the day would come when I would have to make the transition to another life stage.

There is the beauty of reflecting on how I helped others to grow by achieving their goals. I look back on my career and the many struggles I went through and how I overcame each one of them. The ability to find my path and relentlessly pursue it brought joy and a sense of fulfilment, at the very time I thought that life would hold no further enjoyment. It is strange how today I do not see or hear from many of the people I thought were an integral part of my life, yet the memories remain. I believe that people come into our lives for a reason and a season.

> The days of our lives are seventy years; and if by reason of strength they are eighty years, yet their boast is only labour and sorrow; for it is soon cut off, and we fly away.
>
> Psalm 90:10 KJV

As I approached retirement, God provided a partner for me at a time when I least expected him to cross my path. Against a backdrop of losing hope that I would ever meet a person who could change my life, I began to feel excited about sharing my life with another person. I wondered what this new life would mean in my twilight years. I knew that the aging process would bring some of the common conditions associated with deterioration in health, but I wondered, could it also bring beauty?

I was given the insight to write this book after I had written about my personal story of triumph over adversity. Telling my story in my published book called *Hard Truth: Growing out of Adversity* (2021) was incredibly powerful and led me on a journey to make more discoveries. The most beautiful outcome of this publication was the realisation that readers benefited from the power of storytelling and the extent to which it inspired them to see a reflection of themselves. It transpired that the reflective tools I provided were helpful in pointing people in a new direction. I was helped to understand the value of my experiences and how I had become self-aware and reflective. As I read my book again and again, I noticed a phrase that gripped my attention. It was a simple but powerful sentence and was stated thus: 'I exchanged ashes for beauty.' There was no doubt that my life turned to ashes after the sudden and tragic loss of my first husband. With my whole life ahead of me he was suddenly taken away leaving me to cope alone and feeling totally destitute and broken.

I knew that the statement 'exchanging ashes for beauty' was referring to transformation. This idea was reinforced when my sister suggested that a possible topic for my next project could be based on a Bible verse in Isaiah 61:3 which confirmed my sentiment.

> To console those who mourn in Zion, to give them beauty for ashes, The oil of joy for mourning, The garment of praise for the spirit of heaviness; That they may be called trees of righteousness, The planting of the LORD, that He may be glorified.
>
> Isaiah 61:3

I considered the story of Ruth in the Bible who had lost her husband and decided to stay with her mother-in-law Naomi. She chose to travel with her to an unknown land where she could be compared to a stranger in a foreign land. Her life was changed from ashes to beauty after she was spotted by the owner of the field. Boaz spotted her diligence as she was gleaning in the fields, he asked his workmen to leave some of the crops behind for her. That was the day her ashes turned into beauty. She moved from the fields to becoming his wife. I wonder if we recognise that when we are sailing against the tide of life and the storms that offer a number of challenges it is possible to see the beauty in disaster.

It was in seeking a new direction after the publication of *Hard Truth*, that I considered writing a book including the stories of other women alongside my own that would not only be of benefit but would give them access to emotions that they might not have spoken about. This flowed from my own experience of hiding what had happened to me as a young widow and not having the words to explain the depth of my loss.

I am aware that there are many women that go through a plethora of experiences that feel like ashes as it did for me, yet it is always possible to adapt to one's circumstances and become resilient as I did. As people face adversity, they learn how to respond to their struggles in a way that brings a new sense of direction, hope, peace, joy, perseverance, determination and radical transformation.

With these thoughts in mind, I decided to invite ten women to make a contribution to this book by asking them to give me their permission for an interview. I focused on giving them an opportunity to talk about one significant life event that felt like ashes for them but which at the same time became the conduit to their personal growth. I wanted to know about the struggles they had faced and the strategies they had devised as coping mechanisms to respond to their misfortune.

Each participant was given anonymity and the assurance of confidentiality. They were asked to explicitly share their experiences in a way that made sense to them and in a way they could vividly recall. My role was to listen and to validate them without giving an opinion or pronouncing judgement. It was as I listened and recorded the conversations that I used the data to devise storylines and themes. This helped me to see where comparisons and differences in experiences could be made, if at all. It was using the principles of Grounded Theory to analyse data and draw upon the significance of key events that brought the narratives alive. It was helpful to use direct quotes from each participant to give meaning to their stories and allow their voices to be heard. As I conducted the interviews it became apparent that some of the women had not spoken openly to anyone in the context of sharing their burdens, thus, they were often overcome by their emotions. These were the times when I had to stop and allow them to give vent to their raw and unbridled emotions. I was humbled by the fact that these women were able to share parts of themselves with me.

The purpose of this book is to share the experiences of ten women, both positive and negative, and in so doing generate interest in their stories. Realising that my life had been transformed from ashes to beauty I decided to explore their experiences after they had suffered in a way that became very challenging for them. I wanted to know if they had moved 'from ashes to beauty' and if so, how they had achieved it. The women were asked to share personal insight, tools, and tips that other women might find helpful and inspirational. At this point I must say that gender in and of itself was not the main idea, since I realise that men have equally important stories to tell, but I wanted to focus on women because this book was to be a continuation of my personal experiences as a woman with a wealth of personal and professional experiences and knowledge. This was the intersection at which I could see added value as I incorporated and expanded on my first book.

Half of the sample were known to me, and the other half were referred. They came from different backgrounds and cultures, and with different experiences but I used this opportunity to reconstruct a composite picture of what it felt like for them to go through ashes and yet find beauty. It is the richness of their descriptions and the magnitude of their adversity that give encouragement to those who might be struggling to come to grips with similar experiences. I did not attempt to reveal every aspect of their life story but only one significant experience that impacted them and brought about change.

Throughout this book I will be reflecting on their stories and making sense of their verbalisations. In this way I hope to demonstrate how ashes can lead to transformation. Each story contains an element of a transformed life and gives primacy to this theme, reinforcing that an ashes experience is not the end, but it leads to true beauty.

This book also offers a dual metaphor, that of the boat and storm. My intention is to conceptualise the storms that people go through. The storm and the boat dovetails with ashes since one's life can be consumed by fire or water. Both have the propensity for destruction of great magnitude.

How to use this book

This book is intended to be used as a tool for reflection and learning. I suggest that you use the highlights at the end of each story to reflect on your personal experiences. The activities that follow will give you an opportunity to interact with each story bearing your own story in mind. Remember that we are all individuals and the way we approach and solve problems is different, and is related to our values, upbringing, worldview, ethics, cultural norms and spiritual belief system. Try to avoid blame, criticism or negative judgments: instead, see each story as a way of sharing and connecting with the story-giver at a psychological level and from a distance. Pay attention to how each participant overcame and adjusted to the adversity they experienced.

Ultimately, this book offers tools for personal growth and development. To make the most effective use of it, you should consider using a journal to record your thoughts as you answer the questions that are posed at the end of each chapter as food for thought. It is also possible to record your notes in the boxes provided in this book. Whichever method you use make it a meaningful exercise and one where you can apply the lessons you will learn.

Meet the participants

In order to provide anonymity each participant was given a pseudonym to avoid identification.

Trudy: Of Asian-background, in her early thirties. Trudy presented her story as a victim of an airplane crash during her childhood leading to disfigurement and self-loathing.

Jamila: Of African-Caribbean background, Jamila suffered the negative impact of racism and discrimination in the workplace. She was separated from her family during an intense period of suffering.

Davina: Of African-Caribbean background, Davina was overlooked for promotion even though she was overqualified for the position she had applied for. She had no evidence to prove that inequality was responsible but this disappointment impacted her life in ways she did not expect.

Maranda: Of African-Caribbean background, Maranda faced betrayal, financial abuse, separation and loss leading to divorce. She became homeless and felt the sting of rejection and loneliness. As a single parent she was forced to care for her children single-handedly.

Sally: Of white British background, Sally lived with family dysfunction throughout her childhood leading to anxiety and long-term mental health problems. She was sectioned and hospitalised under the Mental Health Act. She attempted suicide several times.

Amina: Of Asian-background, Amina faced domestic abuse, loss, financial abuse and exploitation. As a child her parents did not believe that she could achieve anything. Having lost all of her financial resources through her husband's gambling, infidelity and emotional abuse she found herself on the streets as a single parent and homeless. Failed relationships were an integral part of her unhappiness.

Olivia: Of African-Caribbean background, Olivia's mother suffered from mental illness. She was raised in a residential home for the majority of her childhood. By the age of thirteen she became pregnant leading to rejection and abandonment by her father.

Clarissa: Of African-Caribbean background, Clarissa suffered from burnout, mental health problems, loss of self-esteem, and a loss of friendships. She was unable to study and as a result was forced to abandon her dreams.

Janine: Of white British background, Janine suffered with serious mental health problems and suicidal thoughts/ideation. During her darkest hours she became pregnant and feared that she would not love her baby.

Roseanne: Of African background, Roseanne was separated from her parents because of her choice of faith. Working in a male-dominated environment she suffered with self-doubt, leading to depression and eventually a nervous breakdown following racism and discrimination in the workplace.

CHAPTER ONE

Conceptualising Ashes

And he knew it and said, 'It is my son's coat, an evil beast has devoured him; Joseph is without doubt rent in pieces. And Jacob rent his clothes, and put sackcloth upon his loins, and mourned for his son many days'

Genesis 37:33-34

Ashes is the representation of what is left behind. Going through an "ashes" experience is life-altering. It changes one's perspective so that different lenses are used to make sense of an experience that produces pain. However, there is a possibility that out of the ashes something that is good and enduring can evolve. However, at most times ashes are perceived as faded beauty, leaving nothing but tears, heartache and pain behind. It feels like the residue of what has existed but is now gone. It is a sense of loss, hopelessness, sadness and not being able to see alternatives. It is nothingness and its finality is associated with endings. It is when everything is stripped bare, there is no veneer, no gloss and no covering. In Bible times loss was so severe that people covered themselves in sackcloth and ashes, which was a symbol of mourning, repentance and humility.

We may set out on our destination with high hopes, but these hopes may not be accomplished. We are born into a world that holds promise, yet there comes a time when we must face up to the harsh realities of life. The student who leaves home for university with expectations of gaining a degree may not finish his/her studies for one reason or another. This may bring a sense of failure, disillusionment and disappointment. Yet, it is the steps that are taken next that determine the student's true destination. So it is with all of us. We are on a journey and there are twists and turns, we may travel on rugged terrain, hills or deserts. We may be on the mountain top, or in the valley but we have to know that God is able to do all things for our good. God says:

> For I know the thoughts that I think toward you, saith the LORD, thoughts of peace, and not of evil, to give you an expected end.
>
> Jeremiah 29:11

Conceptualising Beauty

> Favour is deceitful and beauty is vain; but a woman that feareth the Lord, shall be praised.
>
> Proverbs 31:3

Most people tend to conceptualise beauty in terms of what they see on the surface. Philosophers argued that beauty can be subjective and objective. Back in 1976, Hume wrote that *Beauty has no quality in things themselves: It exists merely in the mind which contemplates them; and each mind perceives a different beauty.* The Mona Lisa is considered to be a graphic depiction of a beautiful woman, yet beauty is in the eye of the beholder, what was beautiful was the skill of the artist as he painted the woman. Leonardo da Vinci had only drawn attention to a particular type of beauty. There are other forms of beauty that go unnoticed and undetected by the human eye. This is because we tend to equate beauty with the fairness of a person's skin, the length and colour of their hair, body shape, the colour of their eyes, taste, sight, the clothing they wear, a well-built body, long legs, or even the sound of their voices. This is the stuff that movie stars are made of because they are portraying a certain type of beauty.

Anita Bhagwandas (2023) stated that she had not been able to make a significant shift in her mindset and accept her appearance of a dark skin and being over-sized through lack of understanding of why it felt bad or why she was made to feel bad about the word "ugly". It is more to do with who makes the rules about who is beautiful and who is ugly. She contends that from a young and impressionable age we are taught about the importance of how we should look. In a real sense not living up to other people's expectations of beauty robs us of our confidence and self-worth. Marcus Garvey's (1986) thesis of colonialism and oppression argued that standards of beauty are relentlessly reinforced in authoritative images. These images are incompatible with a black skin and out of reality with African cultural values. We see these images all around us, as we visit museums, in public statues, in churches and other edifices.

When I was growing up in Barbados there were children that had lighter skin complexions than others. They were more likely to be given jobs in banks and placed in trustworthy positions than those with a dark complexion. When I arrived in the United Kingdom, I discovered that this mentality existed then as it does today. It is difficult to get rid of some of the erroneous ideas that people hold on to based on the differences they see and because of the values they hold. The oversized girl who wants to become a ballerina is less likely to be accepted as becoming successful than the girl who is slim and fits in with the notions of other people's expectations of what a ballerina should look like and hence, what constitutes beauty.

Such was the case for an African girl called Michaela DePrince. She was born in Sierra Leone and her original name was Mabinty Bandura. Her father was murdered by rebels during the civil war and her mother died shortly after of starvation. Mabinty was left in an orphanage by her uncle and there she suffered at the hands of her carers because she had a condition that altered the colour of her skin. While being relegated to living in an orphanage she found a newspaper clipping of a ballerina and longed to become like the girl in the picture. As things stood, the notion of becoming a ballerina was way beyond her grasp and out of her reality. Nevertheless, she kept the clipping and clung onto the hope that one day she would become a ballerina.

Mabinty's life changed after she was adopted by a white American couple. One of the biggest changes that adoption brings is a change of name and sense of belonging. In a new environment and under different circumstances Mabinty was given the opportunity to pursue her dream. Her name was changed through adoption, and she was given a new identity. Her book *Hope in a Ballet Shoe* tells of her transformation from an orphan to a famous and graceful ballerina. Her ashes turned into beauty when she rose to fame and became an internationally famous star. After DePrince died suddenly in 2024 at the age of twenty-nine the world mourned her loss; she was referred to as a person who had inspired many young dancers. Her family remembered her as a person with a gorgeous smile. My only regret is that I did not have the opportunity to see her on stage.

We only have to look at DePrince to see that there was a process of moving from ashes to beauty. The caterpillar must move through many stages of metamorphosis before it eventually emerges as a graceful butterfly. The loss we experience begins with pain, desolation and discouragement, but it can change with time and by moving from one stage to another, it is a process that forces us to stay with the pain.

Many people fail to realise that the substance of beauty does not come from without but from within. As mere humans we see on the outside, but it is a good thing that God looks at the heart and not, as we do, on a person's outward appearance. When He was choosing a king for Israel God said to Samuel:

> Do look at his appearance or at his physical stature, because I have refused him. For the LORD does not see as man sees; for man looks at the outward appearance, but the LORD looks at the heart.
>
> 1 Samuel 16:7

It is what we create on the inside that matters most but, in many instances, people make assumptions and judgements about what comprises beauty. It is said that beauty is skin deep which means that we are hesitant to see what lies behind what we instinctively think and feel. Nevertheless, the eye of the beholder is only about what they perceive, since another person may look at the same person or object and see something that is entirely different. We look not only with our eyes but also with our minds and with our souls. The mind gives subtle messages which in turn create ideas that we act on. As a result of what we see, we love or hate, we accept or reject. The person who is beholding has the opportunity to decide if they appreciate what they have seen. The extent to which they are able to value what they see is a matter of perception. In the famous optical illusion of the young and old woman we see one or both of them from the angle of our perception. When we see the young woman, we automatically see beauty and the converse when we see the older woman.

I am reminded of Constance Briscoe's inspiring memoir called *Beyond Ugly* (2007). As one writer said, her story is one that tugs at the heart strings as she tells of the physical and emotional abuse she suffered at the hands of her mother and stepfather during her formative years. Her mother in a fit of twisted rage labelled her "ugly". Constance refused to be silent even though she suffered many beatings, fuelled by the bedwetting which came as a result of the unkind and cruel treatment she received. Her ability to stand up for her rights was in stark contrast to her siblings who became passive. By the age of thirteen she and her siblings were abandoned by their mother. Despite the chaos in her personal life, Constance excelled at school. Motivated to make a new life she went on to study and gained an honours degree in Law and fulfilled her dream to become a barrister. Her story could have had a different ending had it not been for her willpower, determination and strong belief in the beauty that was within. Her story reinforces the beauty that emerges out of the ashes of a painful past when we become motivated and passionate.

The person who is broken, destitute and tattered may not appear to others to be beautiful and yet God has given each one of us something that is unique and different. There are no two people who are alike because the Bible tells us that each hair on our head is numbered. Whatever others may think of us we all go to the same place and have the same fate. We return to dust and ashes. There are no brownie points when it comes to the end of one's life, there are no memories of outward beauty, but the true quest is the beauty we leave behind. We came into life with nothing, and we can take nothing with us. God told Adam that he came from dust and would return to dust (Genesis 3:19). Dust and ashes are inextricably linked since Abraham recognised it when he said to the Lord that he was dust and ashes. Similarly, when Job lost his sons, his oxen, his servants, his shepherds, his houses, everything he possessed was taken away from him, he was reduced to metaphorical ashes. He was stricken with grief; he shaved his head and threw himself face down on the ground and declared:

> … naked I came out of my mother's womb and naked I shall return thither: the Lord gave and the Lord hath taken away; blessed be the name of the Lord.
>
> Job 1:20-21

It takes great faith to reach this level of acceptance and surrender.

Although some people might say that they do not want to be cremated, the fact is that ashes are where we will eventually end up. When we come to the end of life's journey we return to where we came from:

> All go to one place, all are from the dust and to dust all return.
>
> Ecclesiastes 3:20

During our living years, we have the opportunity to go through a process of transformation and restoration. I have a beautiful crystal vase that was broken. I delayed discarding the vase and longed to see it restored to its former beauty. I kept the pieces and one day I had the idea to start glueing it back together again, but my attempts to restore it were futile until I found a craftsman who was able to repair the crystal vase. My joy was unimaginable when I received the repaired crystal vase, there were no leaks, and the water was contained within the vase. Rising from the ashes is concerned with restoration and a return to original beauty.

As I sit in my study I gaze out at the garden and I see beautiful flowers, tall trees that stand proudly in the air and the breeze swaying them from one direction to another. I do not know where the wind comes from or where it is going, but I know that it has an impact on what I can see. At times I also see the wild flowers that grow on the lawn and while they do not belong there, they give colour to the grass. I walk to the park, and I notice the oak trees and the acorns that have fallen to the ground. I think about how acorns become oak trees. When I walk in the park, I see people strolling with their dogs and children playing on the merry-go-round and the swings. It is then that I think of the beauty of youth and strength. I see diversity all around me and I think not only of people but of the beauty of creation, composed of texture, hues, and shades. When I see older people walking with sticks and holding Zimmer frames, I remember that once they were young, vibrant and full of life; they have grown old and are in another phase of their life, as I am. Yet, it is a beautiful time to write a book.

On a grander scale, I think of storms, whirlwinds, earthquakes and fires. They are all devastating. But after they have come to a standstill, there is the beauty of the life that was saved and what remains. In the autumn the leaves turn into glorious colours, yet they fall to the earth and die. But the restoration of nature comes in the spring when the bulbs push up their heads from beneath the ground, the apple blossom trees come back to life in radiant and blooming colours.

Recently I read of a church in Brazil where everything was burned to ashes, but the church was untouched and stood among the ashes. I reflected on how it was possible for a building to remain standing when everything around it had been destroyed by fire and reduced to ashes. The beauty of God and his power to stretch out His hand and save is a mystery we may never fully understand. All of these things cause me to ponder, wonder and give thanks for life. At such times I smile because I am alive, but I know that life even with all its beauty will one day come to an end.

I am reminded of the impressionist artist Pierre-Auguste Renoir whose hands were deformed with arthritis. He suffered untold pain. One day a critic was examining his work and asked him how he could paint with such deformed hands. Renoir confirmed that his hands were deformed and that he felt the pain, but he said with each stroke comes the beauty. It is undoubtedly difficult to go through the pain, but beauty eventually shines through and brings hope.

When I was working I had very little time to pay attention or notice the beauty that was around me. I was too busy to sit down and look intently for beauty, I only tended to see things that were on the surface. It is only as I am reaching my retirement years that I can spend time meditating and thinking of being more appreciative of the world. As Louis Armstrong sang, it is a beautiful world because he could see many things that he loved. The lyrics of the song are shown below.

> I see trees of green
> Red roses too
> I see them bloom
> For me and you
> And I think to myself
> What a wonderful world.
> I see skies of blue
> And clouds of white
> The bright blessed day
> The dark sacred night
> And I think to myself
> What a wonderful world.
> The colours of the rainbow
> So pretty in the sky
> Are also on the faces
> Of people going by
> I see friends shaking hands
> Saying, "How do you do?"
> They're really saying
> I love you
> I hear babies cry
> I watch them grow
> They'll learn much more
> Than I'll ever know
> And I think to myself
> What a wonderful world
> Yes, I think to myself
> What a wonderful world.
> Ooh, yes.

(Louis Armstrong 1967)

CHAPTER TWO

Until the Storm Passes

I was born in Barbados, one of the islands in the Caribbean, where storms and hurricanes are frequent, perhaps we might even say that today they are a part of life. They come with a destructive force, the sea, the wind and the rain can wreak havoc on small communities. In recent years we have heard about hurricanes and tsunamis across the world reaching category four, five and even seven on the scale, killing people, destroying homes, some of the most historical buildings and ruining the life chances of many people and entire communities. These physical storms and hurricanes have a devastating impact on us, and we are no mere match as human beings against the forces of nature.

I am always intrigued by the story of the disciples who set out on a fishing expedition in a boat and were met with a storm. This story is recorded in the gospel of Mark 4: 35-41. Jesus was asleep in the back of the boat. He was tired from an exhausting day, when the winds and the waves came with unrelenting force and threatened to destroy the boat and the fishermen. Fear engulfed them and it looked as if they would perish, but Jesus commanded the winds and the sea to be still, after which he said them, 'Oh Ye of little faith.' They retorted, 'What manner of man is this, that even the winds and the waves obey him.' It is only after the storm that in the calm, we realise the mortal danger we have faced.

I am also reminded of a movie I saw many years ago called *The Perfect Storm* but with a different ending. A boat had set out in a hurricane with a crew of ten. They had left a hurricane behind and went in search of fish off the port of Gloucester, Massachusetts. They were successful in catching thousands of fish. In an attempt to get their catch back to land they met with a powerful weather front and a hurricane which they underestimated. The boat was battered by the winds and the waves. Against their best attempts to solve the many problems they encountered, they found it impossible to survive the onslaught of the winds and the waves. The entire crew lost their lives. I take from this story that not everyone survives the storms of life and not everyone's ashes turn to beauty, but there are those who survive against the odds. My goal is to use ashes and beauty, the boat and the storm from a spiritual perspective to show how we can navigate difficult life events and emerge as beautiful and resilient people.

Being who you are

> Now therefore ye are no more strangers and foreigners, but fellow citizens with the saints, and of the household of God.
>
> Ephesians 2:19

There are many people who want to be like others or assume an alternative identity, they do not value who they are and would prefer to become another person. For one reason or another, they do not see the beauty or the strength that lies within them. While it is not a bad thing to emulate others for the qualities and characteristics they possess, essentially you cannot change who you are unless you go under the knife or engage in some other body- and mind-altering experience. Even then the basic person you are will inevitably remain as your footprint. As we grow older and move into the final stages of life, we remember the younger days and want to retain youthfulness and zest for life for as long as possible. When older women dressed like younger women in the community where I grew up, people would say 'she is mutton trying to look like lamb.' This meant that an older woman was attempting to hide her age by dressing like a younger woman. The quest was to maintain youthfulness for as long as was humanly possible. Yet, I have experienced that with bodily changes, it is impossible to keep going at the same pace and with the same measure of enthusiasm and vigour. We experience many processes of change and although change is not always easy, we learn to cope with and appreciate another stage of life.

Beauty can be defined in different ways. *The Oxford Dictionary* states that it is a combination of qualities, such as shape, colour, or form that pleases the aesthetic senses, especially sight. Yet it may also be associated with something that is pleasurable and elevates the mind and the spirit. The philosophical definition of beauty is related to one's perception and is linked to our emotions as well as our appreciation of what gives us pleasure arising out of our sensations. These kinds of definitions are conditional and are based on what ignites our senses. Another definition found in the Bible is that of 'gentleness and a quiet spirit.'

> Your beauty should not come from outward adornments such as braided hair and the wearing of jewellery and fine clothes. Instead, it should be that of your inner self, the invading beauty of a gentle and quiet spirit which is of great worth in God's sight.
>
> 1 Peter 3:3-4

As mere human beings, we look at what we see on the outside but the Bible states that God looks at the heart. This means that we can turn ashes into beauty by looking after the condition of our hearts and changing our perspective. When King David saw Bathsheba, he desired her for the physical beauty he saw as he gazed at her body. Yet outward beauty is temporary, it is like a flower that blooms, fades and dies. Every living thing must die and return to the earth.

Identity

Being yourself means valuing who and what you are and having a sense of belonging. It is the qualities you possess and harness that makes you unique, giving personhood. Recently, I was walking in a grocery store, and I saw a little girl and perceived that she had Down's syndrome. Children born with this disability are recognisable by their outward features which are distinctive. This little girl was trying to make friends with another child by waving her hands, smiling and trying to speak in order to make a connection with the other child. I saw the beauty, not the disability, because she was expressing the essence of her inner self. She was being authentic. I cannot say how her parents might have felt when they discovered that their daughter had Down's syndrome, but I felt that their ashes had turned into beauty as I saw her personality shining through.

The hope of most if not all parents is to have a child with ten fingers, ten toes, and a heart that beats, with eyes that look at them with wonderment and ears that detect sounds and speech. Yet not all children are born with all of their full faculties and parents may feel disappointed and let down and choose to give up their child for others to foster or adopt. They naturally want all the things that would lead to 'normal' development, but the true test comes when they receive the opposite of what they desired. Strength of character only develops after trial and tribulation. It is only with hindsight and insight that we can truly understand the process that helps us to overcome obstacles as we move beyond ashes to beauty. The story of Robert Hoge, the author of *Ugly*, (2013) examines why we need to own our own faces. Born with a deformity, he was rejected by his mother, by people in his community and by his peers. He made the choice to own his face, in other words the reality of his identity. He was able to say, 'I knew I was ugly, but everyone is uglier than they think. We are all more beautiful too. We all have scars only we can own.' (Hoge 2013:182)

The life story of Corrie Ten Boom (1971), a Dutch watchmaker and Christian woman, provides a powerful example of what the quality of beauty looks like from the inside. She was instrumental in her mission to help many Jews escape the Nazi Holocaust during World War II. In her book *The Hiding Place*, she tells of her ordeal and the lengths to which she went to save others. In order to move from ashes to beauty we must be willing to make sacrifices that have a cost and a price tag. Inevitably the sacrifice may mean giving up comfort, it may require self-denial, it may mean being attuned to the needs of others and it may mean finding the true reason of why God has placed us on planet earth, that is to say, our purpose.

Suffering and Healing, the Human Paradox

One of the biggest existential and most perplexing questions that people find impossible to answer is why we have to suffer. They ask what is the reason for human suffering, and do not necessarily see any beauty in it until they have gone through an experience that brings them to the end of their limited resources. Suffering is one of the most difficult concepts to understand. In order to answer this question, we must go back to the beginning of creation. It was not God's intention that we should suffer, but we are told in Genesis chapter 3 that after Adam and Eve had been disobedient, they were told that Eve's sorrows would be greatly multiplied in childbirth and that Adam would have to work by the sweat of his brow. There would be thorns and thistles, they would have to eat food from their own sweat and go through hard toil until the day they died. Pain, suffering and death were to be an inevitable part of life. Therefore, death, is the one thing that we cannot circumvent, evade or change. This is where we first hear of an ashes experience that came as a result of jealousy and led Cain to kill his brother Abel. In the book of Genesis, we also read about the deception of Jacob who stole his brother's birthright, egged on by his mother. There is sibling rivalry caused by favouritism leading to jealousy. Modern-day families grapple with the same issues, but forgiveness can break the cycle of broken bonds.

Life is a beautiful symphony and a gift, but the paradox is that we often lose sight of the beauty because it is difficult to see beyond pain and suffering. Suffering has a way of blurring our vision and shaking our confidence, particularly when we reach the point of rock bottom and all we can see is ashes. It diminishes the happiness, peace, and joy that we desire to gain out of life. It is at times like these that we lose sight of God's purpose for our lives because we are overtaken by discouragement. The truth is that for as long as we live, suffering will come in many forms. Some of it may come as a result of ignorance and disobedience, some of it through risk-taking behaviours, the illicit use of alcohol and drugs, the dereliction of duty on the part of parents and those in powerful positions. Some of our sorrows may come through violation of God's laws, some of it at the hands of others and some of our own making and as a result of poor health choices we make, or even health conditions that are beyond our control resulting from genetics. In some instances, our faith may be sorely tested as we go through suffering that is not of our own making. Sorrow and affliction may come to us as a result of natural disasters, mental health problems, loss of a family member or friend, or trauma caused by the abusive acts of others resulting in emotional turmoil.

Human relationships are an area where we suffer most because of the emotional fallout it causes when they disintegrate. We were created to enjoy and treasure human relationships, but it is only when they break down that we suffer in a number of ways. Human suffering includes, but is not limited to, mental health issues, separation, loss, child abuse, rape, domestic abuse, exploitation, self-loathing, self-harm, suicide and addictions of many kinds.

Aretha Franklin was first sexually abused at the age of twelve. It was a secret and a burden that she carried for her entire life. With a deeply religious father, and a mother who had left the family home because of domestic abuse, Aretha found herself alone and withholding her speech. She had her first child at the age of thirteen. As an adult she gravitated towards a man of ill-repute who consistently violated her physically, verbally and emotionally. Despite her misfortune she became known for her talent and was called the Queen of soul. Her contribution to the work of Dr Martin Luther King Jr. set her apart as a legend of her time. When the dark thoughts came, she was overwhelmed with guilt, self-blame and self-loathing. Her response was to turn to alcohol, but her religious background brought her back to where she had started and gave her the survival strategies to cope with the abuse she had suffered.

There are many examples of ashes and beauty we can draw on to widen our understanding of what it both feel and looks like. For example, Mother Teresa's work among the most down and out people on the streets of Calcutta teaches us that beauty does not exist in makeovers, but in the simple things of life. She told the story of a boy she had rescued and taken to a children's home. He was given a bath, clean clothing and everything that he needed, but soon after he ran away from the children's home. He was rescued a second time, and once again he ran away and was found again. The sisters were asked to follow the boy and bring him back to the children's home. On questioning him they discovered that he was returning to his mother. His mother had put some stones under a tree and there she was cooking the remains of what she had salvaged from the waste bins. Asked why he was returning to this life, the boy said, 'But this is my home, because this is where my mother is.' That is essentially what belonging is about, it is where the heart is and it is where we feel a real sense of connectedness. Even though the boy had nothing in terms of materialism, he had a strong sense of identity with his mother, she was all he had and it was what he prized over and above a bath and clean clothing. The beauty in this boy's story was his love for his mother and his need to be with her despite the fact that she had nothing to offer him.

The stories in this book hold many experiences where the participants felt that life had dealt them a terrible blow, some had traumatic experiences that led them down roads of uncertainty, fear and failure, yet the true story was how they became resourceful and resilient in the face of incredible adversity. All of the women were facing their own challenges. Each of them needed to find a way to survive. This is when suffering was paradoxical because it was intertwined with hidden beauty. It is the time to remember that God's purpose is to bring healing and restoration from the seemingly senseless suffering we go through.

The Bible story of the widow who had lost her son and everything she had demonstrates how God reframed her picture. The widow's son had died and Elijah the prophet brought him back to life, but she was told to make preparation and leave her home because of a famine that would last for seven years. The woman followed Elijah's instruction, leaving her household and going to live in the land of the Philistines, where she remained for seven years. At the end of the seven years, the woman returned home and appealed to the king to repossess her house and her fields. On hearing her story, the king restored her house and land and everything that was hers, including the produce of her fields. 2 Kings 8:1-6. When we reframe a picture it gives us a second chance to transform our lives.

In my personal times of suffering, I discovered that the quest for beauty was a process that I had to go through. My best strategies were to first possess a spirit of audacity. When everything was against me and everything pointed to failure, I stood up and fought back by rising to every challenge I faced. The spirit of audacity would not allow me to give up or be silent but to fight with determination. In my heart of hearts, I knew that I had to adapt and change around my circumstances. This is the essence of resilience.

Second, I stepped up to the plate – what I saw on my plate was discouragement and fear, so I prayed hard to overcome the fear. I realised that I had two choices, sink or swim, so I swam. In the interest of self-preservation, I hid what had happened to me and I did not talk openly about the pain I was suffering. I began to study and eventually I was able to help many others along the way.

Stepping up to the plate was the best thing I ever did, because it allowed me to take personal responsibility and move in a new direction. Becoming courageous was my response to intense suffering. So, what does it look like to be courageous? It is when fear looms large like an albatross over your head, but you refuse to sink into despair, despondency and paralysis.

Third, I reclaimed and reframed my experience. The notion of reclaiming and reframing was a powerful strategy for contextualising my experience as a black woman. I reclaimed the right to life, I preferred to live rather than die. I reclaimed my faith and it became the foundation on which I built self-belief and the right to be who I am. It was my faith that drove the narrative of strength over weakness. It was my faith that gave me hope and the will to survive. I know that I would not have achieved success if I had not exercised faith and trust in God's providence.

I became resilient by reclaiming the right to be different. Even though it was difficult, at times I chose to stand alone and for what I believed in. I chose to go places where people said or thought that it was impossible to go. I did not look at the mountain, but how I could climb it, I did not look at the giant but how I could conquer it. The more we look at mountains and giants the more we pale into insignificance. I chose to become independent and remained a widow for forty-seven years, but I had to endure the pain of loneliness.

Reframing the picture was how I saw the world through different lenses. I contained my thought processes and moved away from self-blame, self-pity and negativity to positive thinking. God provides the strength to those who go through suffering and he promises that his grace is sufficient (2 Corinthians 12:9).

I rebuilt my life when it appeared that my future was bleak. The idea of rebuilding one's life at the same time as going through suffering can sometimes mean going against the grain, but there are choices I made at the time that built the foundation for a strong structure. Against the odds, I became strong not in my own strength but in God's strength and according to the purpose he gave me. I became passionate and focused and that was the recipe for my success and strength of character. I would say that at the time, I did not know that I was searching for beauty, but I knew it as I grew older and was able to reflect on my life.

Do you sometimes feel that your suffering is too much to bear? Are you sometimes crushed by the struggles of life that weigh you down? How do you respond during times of discouragement?

It is encouraging to know that Christ was more determined than ever to overcome so that we can conquer and overcome our battles. His determination was so strong that he was able to move beyond the crushing weight of pain. Such courage, such fortitude, such singlemindedness should allow you to know that healing is possible. Whatever we are suffering we can be sure that God has made a better way, but if we do not find the solution to suffering in our lifetime, we will surely find it in the life to come. Jesus gave us the assurance that He has gone to prepare a place for us. His sentence did not end at that point but continued:

> If I go to prepare a place for you, I will come again and receive
> you unto myself that where I am there you will be also.
>
> John 14:3

There is comfort and reassurance in this verse of scripture because it places emphasis on a positive outcome and on certainty.

Pain with Patience

> I didn't think then of all the misery, but of the beauty that still remains. My advice is go outside, to the fields, enjoy nature and sunshine, go out and try to capture happiness. Think of all the beauty that is still left in and around you and be happy.
>
> ANNE FRANK

The quest for beauty requires patience. One of the most difficult experiences in life is to go through the kind of pain that never stops. It is almost impossible to focus on beauty when you are in physical, emotional or psychological pain. Misery hangs over your head like an albatross with its huge wingspan. Suddenly you realise that you are no match for this predator from which you cannot escape.

In 1976 I suddenly fell and sustained a back injury. At that time, it was common for doctors to advise bed rest. I was bedridden for almost three months; the physical pain was difficult to bear. However, I eventually recovered and was able to get on with most tasks. Some years later the pain returned, and I discovered that I was losing the ability to do many simple household chores, such as standing at the sink, hoovering, lifting and carrying shopping, gardening and driving. I lost the ability to stand or walk for long periods. I was often sitting in front of doctors complaining about the debilitating pain in my lower back radiating down my legs.

With scans, it was discovered that I had two protruding discs at the base of my spine. My worst fear was that I would end up in a wheelchair and lose my independence. Time after time I prayed that God would take away the pain, but it only got worse. I was living my life in perpetual physical pain. After having injections in my spine that did not work to my benefit, there were only two alternatives open to me, surgery or pain management medication. The fact is that all my work required me to sit at the computer or to stand and give presentations. It was a heavy burden, because it threatened to take away my livelihood. As I got older, the pain increased and became debilitating. It was a constant reminder of my frailty. Although I did not consider myself to have a disability, I had one because the pain interrupted my work, causing me to frequently pause, and to seek medical intervention.

For more than fifty-seven years I have been in pain, albeit at different times and with different intensities. It was an endless cycle of pain. This is the intersection where God gave me the oil of gladness and where I moved from ashes to beauty. Bearing pain without complaining led to patience which came with a high level of dependency on God's grace to see me through each day.

Alongside other interventions, I have had to manage the pain with medication but without becoming dependent on it. I have learnt how to take care of my body with exercise and diet. I have learnt how to ask for help and how to patiently wait for the right type of support. It was not until I was almost in my retirement years that God sent me a dedicated husband who is my rock and who is my steadfast help. I can depend on him to attend to all the tasks that I cannot manage. Patience requires waiting without knowing how long the waiting period will be. I was amazed when an osteopath recently told me that she admired my courage, bravery and strength of character.

I cannot compare my pain with the pain that Jesus suffered on his way to and on the cross of Calvary, but I know that with patience he overcame it and rose victoriously from the grave. I cannot say with any certainty that my physical pain will end, but I know that my Redeemer lives and that one day He will give me a crown of beauty. When we are in pain, God has promised to have compassion on us and comfort us.

> Praise be to the God and Father of our Lord Jesus Christ, the Father of compassion and the God of all comfort, who comforts us in all our troubles, so that we can comfort those in any trouble with the comfort we ourselves receive from God.
>
> 2 Corinthians 1:3-4

Paul the Apostle wrote about a thorn in his flesh; although we are not told what it was, we know that he pleaded with God to remove it, but he was told that God's grace was sufficient in weakness.

My transformation came when I refused to allow pain to define my character, it came when I refused to complain, it came when I refused to take invasive action that might have made my situation worse. Without a guarantee that an operation would improve my condition I was able to wait for a word from God and it came when God sent the support that I needed to change my perspective and give me the courage to bear the never-ending pain. There are many people who are living in some form of pain, it might be physical, emotional or psychological. I take courage from Trudy, who graciously spoke to me in an interview for this book. The insight she gave into how her character was developed through patience is of key importance and shows the process of moving from ashes to beauty.

Trudy's Story: Trial by Fire

Beauty for me was a big thing, I grew up thinking that how I looked mattered, but I no longer look for comments such as you look beautiful. Does people telling you that you look beautiful validate you? No! because I don't live for those comments, I live for transparency. I'm done hiding.

When Trudy was eight years old, she was travelling on an aircraft with her parents and brother when suddenly the aircraft caught on fire in the skies. In a split second, she lost everything, her parents, brother and life as she knew it. Her safety, security and her identity were shattered into a million pieces. Her well-ordered life literally turned to ashes as her skin was engulfed by flames in the sky. Following this accident, she went through endless surgeries where surgeons reconstructed her face and body. While in the hospital the nurses were kind. She did not look at mirrors and hence did not have a conception of her true image, until she was finally discharged, and returned to her extended family and the outside world. Her life was far from normal as she experienced bullying, name-calling, discrimination at school and in the community where she lived. The response of others to the way she looked led to agonising social isolation and loneliness. She states:

When I went back into the wider community the way I looked was unacceptable to others. I was called names such as ugly, Freddie Kruger, and people crossed the road just in case they would catch how I looked.

As a result of the response to her facial and body disfigurement, Trudy began to internalise what she heard about her outward appearance. When family members told her that she was beautiful she dismissed these comments and refused to believe or accept that it could be true. Trudy felt unable to turn to others for help because she was told to ignore those who were the source of her emotional pain. She woke up every day thinking that it would be better if she died and did not want to exist anymore. It was not only the physical pain, but the emotional torment she faced every day as she tried to rebuild her life. Trudy's experience was bitter and agonising because she did not like herself and refused to believe that she was a beautiful child.

The Mystery of Survival

It was after many years that Trudy was able to exchange ashes for beauty. It was after she was introduced to an organisation that supports people with visible differences that she gained the strength to see beauty through different lenses. With support to speak from her site of oppression, she was able to become an ambassador for others who were suffering the pain of being different. She stated:

It wasn't until I began to realise that the beauty, I could see in them is what I needed to see in myself.

The key to change was self-acceptance because she realised that we are:

Living in a world where beauty is glorified but it was finding the tools to deal with my ordeal.

For Trudy, it was the realisation that it is important to find the right tools to deal with internal pain and to implement them. She stated:

I had security and then it was gone, as an adult I could not use the same coping strategies.

There was more disappointment to come because at the age of twenty-six Trudy was diagnosed with renal failure and had to live on dialysis. This disappointment came as she was in the midst of completing a degree. Of this experience, Trudy stated that her developing sense of confidence was once again tested. She had to ask how she could turn her ashes into beauty. One key to facing the pain caused by her ashes was to realise that self-awareness and self-acceptance are crucial. Self-awareness was how she began to take control of her life, by managing her emotions to get through tough situations. She stated that for most people, *'there is a tendency to suppress their emotions,'* but today, she is able to allow herself to cry as opposed to hiding in the shadows which is what she did as a child.

Trudy's observation is that as children we have *'our own internal knowledge'* which allows us to feel what is right, but once we have been conditioned on how to think and how to feel, everything we first knew is taken away from us through a process of eradicating what we first knew; the instincts we are given at birth disappear and we assume different ways of knowing and understanding the world. She concluded that:

It is the social constructs to which we conform that stop us from being who we are.

The discovery of her personhood is what eventually led to a better understanding of herself, a higher purpose in suffering, reclaiming her voice and becoming an ambassador for those who are marginalised because they are disfigured in some way. No longer focusing on physical beauty, Trudy began to see that outward appearance is not intended to take precedence over internal beauty. This thinking opened the door to self-confidence so that she no longer needed to rely on validation from others, hiding under the umbrella of pleasant and sometimes contradictory comments and endless makeovers. It also opened the door to self-knowledge which comes from within. Trudy referred to self-knowledge as:

Knowing that the answers we seek are from within, wisdom is from within this is spiritual wisdom.

Trudy's transformational journey to emotional beauty is to be fully surrendered. She said:

I have left it to God, whatever role he has designed for me I will step into it and align myself with His will. I do not know what will happen in the future, but I am ready at this moment to do His Divine work with my voice and allow myself to be used. Jesus's message was sacrifice, we will never understand it, we don't have to have our hands nailed to the cross, but we can take these elements for the greater good. Love, compassion, and acceptance, everyone has it within them and we should celebrate it. We don't come into the world with a manual but we learn. We need to start being kind and that for me is really important and it is what leads to beauty.

Trudy loves the quote that is often attributed to Mahatma Gandhi because she understands that it is only by showing love and kindness that we can change and move from ashes to beauty.

> You must be the change you want to see in this world.
>
> Mahatma Gandhi

A commentator said that Ghandi's message was to embody the values and principles we wish to see in the world. He also said that the best way to find yourself is to lose yourself in the service of others.

Reflecting on Trudy's journey – Abundance

There are different types of pain that we all suffer; good things can happen to bad people and bad things can happen to good people. Trudy's journey caused her to grow in ways that many people would find difficult to understand and they might even reach the point of giving up. As I interviewed Trudy, I knew that she had incredible power to overcome the setbacks she had faced throughout her life-long journey, beginning with her childhood experience of losing everything. When she eventually woke up to the reality that her parents and her only brother had perished in the flames, as the sky was shattered so were her dreams. As it stood, her life was nothing but rubble, but she did not allow her difficulties to define her as a person. Instead, with time and a lot of personal work, she developed the skills that were hidden, namely, the ability to communicate effectively and with a voice of compassion. One can see inner beauty as she speaks single-mindedly about her struggles without focusing on misfortune. She used her experiences to search for a higher cause and to support those without a voice. Going through many operations and facing renal failure she has been able to see herself as one who is willing to be used by God for a higher purpose – that of service. It is for this reason that she has experienced abundance in ways that many people with material possessions do not achieve. This is because abundance is given as a gift from God.

The concept of abundance is not to do with material possessions, class, or status but it is more to do with how we allow God to take the broken and shattered pieces of our lives and mend them beyond all recognition. It is when we are given over and above what we expect to receive. When Jesus said that he came to give life more abundantly, he was not referring to material possessions but a life of joy and peace. The apostle Paul referred to abundance as God supplying all our needs according to his riches in glory.

Taking Personal Responsibility

Trudy learnt how to take personal responsibility and how to stand up for herself. She knows that beauty is only skin deep and does not quantify the worth of a person or their character. In this regard, she is transparent and is willing to stand up for what she believes to be honest, and true. A person's version of beauty is determined by what they feel about themselves and how they react to other people's negative comments when their distress is greatest. In my estimation, Trudy stands out as a person of beauty because she is not depending on others to validate and give consent to who she is. It is possible to be admired for the qualities we possess, but of ourselves, we do not create human qualities, but they are given to us by an abundant God who wants us to see people as they are and not as we would like them to be.

In later life Trudy suffered with a serious and life-threatening illness, she also lost the opportunity to study. She was able to move beyond her ashes to find beauty.

Each part of the body must work in unison, similar to a cog in a wheel, where all the parts fit together neatly, causing the wheel to operate efficiently. This begs the question of how we can take care of the spiritual, physical, emotional, and psychological aspects of our entire being, realising that if one part of the body is not fully synchronised it impacts every other part of our functioning.

In the context of Trudy's journey, in every aspect of pain, I can return to my personal experiences of both emotional and physical pain and see that I too have overcome in areas of my life where I felt that it was impossible to overcome, but by adopting simple child-like trust it was possible to do so. It was by asking for the patience to push through and endure the pain that led to Trudy's transformation. We cannot reach the stage of beauty unless we go through the pain, neither can we escape the disappointment and the heartache that is a natural part of life unless we choose to ignore or sidestep it. Trudy chose to be grateful for her voice and uses it to express who she is, that is to say, her unique identity. She said:

> I was not born to fit in, I was born to stand out. I am grateful that I have a voice, whatever you have use it to express who you are.

Highlights based on Trudy's journey

- Remind yourself daily that beauty comes from within, not from without
- Remember that God has already made provision for whatever help you need
- Look for the raven it will always bring a flower
- Divide your body into four sections, the spiritual, physical, emotional and psychological, and work to consistently nourish each segment of your body

- By all means admire others for the value they bring, but prize and value yourself and your worth
- Take personal responsibility for your thoughts, your actions and your behaviour
- Make something beautiful of your life by helping others and by being of service.

Food for Thought

1) Use your journal or the box below to record the beauty you see in yourself.
2) What, if any, steps can you take to cultivate a sense of beauty as you are going though pain whether it is physical, emotional, spiritual, or psychological?

CHAPTER THREE

Facing the Storm

Therefore, whoever hears these sayings of Mine, and does them, I will liken him to a wise man who built his house on a rock: and the rain descended, the floods came, and the winds blew and beat on that house: and it did not fall, for it was founded on the rock. But everyone who hears these sayings of Mine, and does not do them, will be like a foolish man who built his house on the sand, and the winds blew and beat on that house; and it fell. And great was its fall.

Matthew 7: 24-27

The wisdom contained in the parable of the two houses came directly from Jesus as he gave a sermon on the mount of Olives. He spoke to those who gathered to hear His words about the importance of navigating the unpredictability of storms. Jesus likened the builder to those who chose to build a strong foundation as those who are wise, but those who build their house on the sand as foolish. He compared himself to the rock, the solid foundation. The other implications of this parable are that when the storms of life come if we do not listen to the advice we are given and build a strong foundation all our efforts will come to nothing. The storm symbolises the challenges and adversities that we encounter during life's journey.

As I sit in my study there is a storm raging outside, I feel comfortable to be under the shelter of a roof as I hear parts of the guttering and roof shaking. At times I feel afraid, particularly as the storm started when it was daylight, and it is now night. As the shadows fall, I hear the boisterous winds and the rain beating relentlessly on the entire structure of my home. I am aware of my insignificance against the natural forces of the storm. I cannot control them; therefore, my best action is to make sure that that I close the windows and doors. I am relying on the fact that the house is built on a strong foundation and a secure reinforced structure. This notion of the house and the storm explores the characteristics of both, shedding light on the elements in the sermon on the mount that contribute to either disaster or survival.

As a child I lived in a house that was called a Chattel house. They were wooden structures raised above the ground and were naturally susceptible to high winds. During the stormy season care had to be taken to protect them against rain, falling debris and damage from falling trees. My first encounter with a storm was in 1955. My mother had just given birth to my brother and arrived home as the storm was looming. People on the entire island were being evacuated to places of safety. I remember walking to a local school as the wind lifted trees from their roots. I remember entering the school for shelter and although as a child it felt like fun, it was serious. The only reason we could find refuge in the school was because it was built on a strong foundation, making it a safe place to shelter from the storm.

> Sometimes God calms the storm, at other times he lets the storm rage and calms his child.
>
> LESLIE GOULD

The serious nature of Jesus' parable also shows that there are consequences for those who disobey God's commandments. A house needs to be constructed and reinforced with sturdy materials to withstand the relentless assault and battering of the wind and rain. Its resilience is crucial in preventing water from penetrating the roof during stormy weather. The house is capable of standing firm, but it must be built on rock to reinforce the structure against an unforeseen force that can cause substantial damage, namely subsidence. The foundation must be built on rock, but the house that is built on sand will collapse. At the seaside I enjoy watching children building castles in the sand. Once the sea is in ebb tide, seaward, they resemble beautiful structures and can be described as a work of art.

However, when the flow tide comes in the sandcastles simply disappear and with it the hard work and effort in building them.

When a boat is at sea there are several elements of its frame that are critical. The captain must build the boat of strong material in the same way as a carpenter would build a house. The materials they use must be of good quality and durable to withstand the storm. The wheel is the instrument of navigation, steering the boat towards the captain's intended destination. The captain represents an individual facing life's storm, he holds the pivotal role in navigating the waters. The captain's skills, knowledge and emotional control during a time of disaster become paramount in determining the journey's outcome, especially when confronted with setbacks that could lead to disaster and the ultimate destruction of the boat, its passengers and himself.

Two integral elements connected to the boat and the storm are the lighthouse and the anchor. The lighthouse serves as a guide, illuminating the path through the darkness of the storm. As night falls and challenges intensify, the lighthouse becomes the beacon of hope that aids the captain in finding the way forward. When the time comes, the anchor, firmly held by solid rock, reduces the risk of drifting aimlessly in the turbulent sea. It provides stability and resilience against the unpredictable forces, grounding the boat amidst the storm's chaos. This metaphor emphasises the importance of being well-equipped to face life's challenges, much like a boat is designed to navigate stormy waters. The journey may be fraught with losses caused by various tempests, but the boat's construction, navigation tools, guiding lights and anchor offer survival in times of disaster. Like an anchor Jesus keeps us from drifting or being tossed backward and forward when we face challenges in our lives. Priscilla Owens wrote the Hymn "Will Your Anchor Hold":

We have an anchor that keeps the soul, steadfast and sure while the billows roll; fastened to the Rock which cannot move, grounded firm and deep in the Saviour's love!

Setting the Sails

The term setting the sails dates back to the 15th century and was a nautical term used to describe seamen who hoisted the sails in preparation for a sea voyage. In advance of setting out, the sails were set to provide force against the winds and propel the boat across the ocean; skill was needed to turn the sails towards the winds. The role of the captain was to constantly move the sails to give the ship direction, allowing it to move towards its chartered course. The winds on a sea voyage are similar to the winds of life which can blow us to places where we do not want to go. They may take us far off course and hence as the captain there is a need to set the sails.

Ultimately, it is the captain's ability to adapt to what is going on around him, it is his inner strength to navigate and stay on course which determines whether those on the boat will emerge from the storm battered or strengthened, or if they will emerge at all. The quest to survive the storm is what ultimately moves it to its intended destination and new-found beauty. It is certain that life's winds may be uncontrollable because we do not know when or where they will come from or where they are going. *We have no control over the wind because it blows where it wishes, you hear its sound, but you cannot tell where it comes from or where it goes.*

> The wind bloweth where it listeth, and thou hearest the sound thereof, but canst not tell whence it cometh, and whither it goeth: so is every one who is born of the Spirit.
>
> John 3:8 NKJV

The same concept applies to life, because we do not know where our challenges may come from or where they will end, but when we are born of the spirit, we will trust God to take us through the winds and storms to safe harbour.

Paul the apostle had an experience of a sea journey as he was being escorted as a prisoner on a ship along with others on board. It happened that while they were on the Adriatic Sea they were caught in a shipwreck. This story of the shipwreck is relevant to my discussion because all on board met with violent winds until they feared that they would die. The fear was so great that they cast the anchors out of the stern. During the shipwreck it appeared certain that they would perish. But Paul encouraged the prisoners to eat and thereafter to lighten the load on the boat. None of them lost their lives because they hoisted up the main sail to the wind and made towards the shore.

> When the ship ran aground, the forepart stuck fast and remained unmovable, but the hinder part was broken with the violence of the waves.
>
> Acts 27:41

A well-known pastor told a story of four men who, on a sunny and pleasant day, decided to take a trip out to sea in a boat. A time came when they decided to leave the boat and deep dive. They put the anchor down but while they were away the boat drifted and sank. When they began to swim back to the place where they had anchored the boat, it had disappeared and they found themselves in the deep blue ocean struggling for their lives against the elements of the winds and the storm. Two of the swimmers were overtaken by the turbulent waves and lost their lives. The lesson in this story for me is that a combination of factors can alter the course of one's life: it might be the wind, it might be the sea, and it might be that the anchor is on shallow ground, it might be the vessel in which we are travelling has a leak. It may not be our intention to be tossed by every wind of misfortune, but setting the sails and making adjustments will give us a fighting chance. After the storm has subsided, some people are able to get up, dust themselves off and fight for their survival and others are not. The question is what propels us to keep going?

> The secret to overcoming a storm is to 'start by doing what is necessary, then do what is possible; and suddenly you will do what is impossible.
>
> AUTHOR UNKNOWN

Sally's Journey Into the Unknown

As Sally told her story the metaphor of the boat and the storm came to me as a point of revelation. Her journey through the tumultuous landscape of mental illness could be likened to the devastation we see during a storm.

> *My dad was bipolar. And we lived in quite difficult circumstances. It was a bit of a pressure-cooker environment, because you know, he would get ill and, that was always kind of a really tough experience to go through. And I think that I was angry towards his illness. I didn't direct it at him because I knew it wasn't his fault. But I think I was frustrated with our family situation and the way our life kept falling apart and we'd have to rebuild again as a family and that cycle just went on a normal stream during my childhood and my teenage years. I had a period where I was relatively stable, but then when I was 27, the bipolar started and then that's when the roller-coaster journey started. So very deep depressions. I mean, debilitating depressions.*

Sally grew up in a dysfunctional family and what she termed a 'pressure-cooker environment'. She grappled with intense emotions and the pervasive shadow of bipolar disorder. Her roller-coaster existence truly began during her childhood when she was living in a household where there was disorder, dysfunction and chaos. Her father suffered with bipolar disorder, and she took on many of the symptoms he displayed of manic depression. She felt angry and out of control because there was a lack of consistency and stability in her life.

By the age of twenty-seven Sally was married, but she experienced several mental breakdowns beginning during her adolescent years. Consequently, she was diagnosed with bipolar disorder. Her subsequent journey was marked by episodes swinging between debilitating depression and euphoric mania, leading to many crises that resulted in more than one overdose. She perceived her life as meaningless and of little or no value and took steps to end it. Sally was sectioned under the Mental Health Act and detained in hospital on and off for several years. She suffered from two types of depression, one was manic or what she termed 'mania'. With this condition, she went into a deep state of depression. She experienced extreme emotions and as a result lost many friends. Reflecting on this time she stated:

> *I believed that I was the root of all evil and I believed that I didn't deserve to be alive. I thought that I was a monster that just devoured people's positivity and I was in such a negative place that I felt that I was almost poisonous, and I just did not deserve to be here.*

The other mental health state she experienced was euphoria. She explained that this end of the spectrum of her illness caused her to believe that she was in a perfect world. All of her problems disappeared, and she was given to bouts of extreme spending. She felt as if she had unbelievable super-powers and life had new meaning. She felt invincible, believing that she could communicate with the universe and planet earth. She said:

> *I had delusions of all sorts of things which seemed real, but it was total and utter euphoria.*

Sally states that her experience of mental illness led her on a turbulent collision with death. This was a storm that shattered her life, causing her to lose her husband, friends, her home and a sense of purpose and meaning. Finding herself in the depths of despair, Sally's life seemed irreparably broken, akin to ashes scattered by the wind of her intense emotions. The darkness within her led to feelings of unworthiness. The despair she encountered threatened to consume any semblance of positivity, driving her to believe that she was worthless and did not deserve the gift of life.

However, from the ashes of despair emerged remarkable transformation, it was a movement from despair to beauty. Sally's healing process was slow and arduous, involving strong medication with all its side effects, but it was her persistent effort to rebuild her life that brought change. She was able to say:

> *I am not riding the stormy sea anymore, I have reached a level of peace and stability and I have reached a stage of contentment and gratitude, so I am thankful that I have survived it all.*

In her new-found strength, Sally discovered that returning to art gave her a sense of purpose. It was as if her love of art brought deliverance. The change of deliverance from mental illness reminded her of how precious life is and how we need to be grateful even in the darkest hours. She said:

I like to remind myself of how precious life is, if I can say that I am grateful that I have two legs, that I can stand at my easel and I can pray I will be grateful. I am grateful if the sun isn't shining, and we have got the rain. I can be thankful for the sun, but I can nourish the shade. I am thankful for my relationships, for my friendships, the people in my life that nourish me, I am grateful that I no longer get any negative intrusive thoughts.

Support of friends was key to her healing. She acknowledged that in the midst of her storm friends came to her aid and helped her to overcome self-doubt and fear because she could not see a way out of the storm, but her confidence was put to the test when she defied negative thinking. She said:

When my friends told me that I had a fantastic career I would say no! It's over, that's done, and I will never get back to it, but with their insistence and support I started to believe them, and it turned out that they were right. I only gained insight when I came out of an episode. When you are mentally ill, your brain tricks you into believing negative thoughts, it hijacks your brain, and it gives you a very narrow perspective. Even when you feel as if you are being hijacked there is hope of release from negative emotions.

Gaining the victory over negative thoughts allowed Sally to emerge from her storm as a source of encouragement for others, particularly those who had been hospitalised for many years and could not find their way out of their sea of despair. She became 'empathic, sympathetic and non-judgmental.' Her journey from darkness to light allowed her to rediscover the simple pleasures, a sentiment she ardently expresses:

I only gained insight when I came out of an episode. The fact that I am stable now and am able to enjoy life, in that a sound mind has given me a great sense of being able to enjoy life.

Reflecting on Sally's Journey

The notion of the pressure-cooker environment is a way of describing mounting tension that is about to explode. In order to release the pressure, the valve must be released to reduce the mounting pressure inside the cooker so as to avoid an explosion. Those in charge of the cooker must know how and when to reduce the pressure. During her childhood, Sally lacked parents with the ability to reduce the pressure she was feeling internally. Her father's illness meant that he was incapable of offering her the care, support and empathy she desperately needed. Therefore, instead of feeling compassion for him she resorted to anger, blame and uncontrollable emotions that became destructive.

During Sally's long and enduring mental illness, she attempted suicide on many occasions. Her wish to end her life was evidence of her inability to master her thoughts. Without a port in her storm, she had no hiding place, no cover from the storm, no anchor or lighthouse to relieve her melancholy spirit. The psychological pain, that began in her childhood, was under-girded by the level of tension, disruption and dysfunction she was constantly exposed to in the environment where she existed.

She was traumatised but had no help to deal with her emotions during the early stages of her life, as numerous attempts were made to turn the dial back to reset her life. To have described her home as a pressure cooker signalled the tension and explosive nature of her upbringing that led to anger. Under this condition she was drifting aimlessly until she met her husband. However, unresolved family conflict escalated to boiling point and had a destructive impact on her marriage, friendships and the loss of her home. Without a faith to resort to she was in perpetual anger and resistance. Her inability to find order and put her life into perspective encouraged a downward spiral.

Yet, the significance of Sally's journey lies in the profound transformation she underwent. It was her quest to survive her illness that she states became her salvation. Her story teaches us that we have the capacity to rebuild our lives even when we are faced with struggles that are harsh, just like the winds that batter the boat until it is reduced to nothing.

Sally's way of escape came through her creativity and love of art; it became a therapeutic lighthouse, guiding her through the tangled maze of her mental health struggles to emerge as an artistic work of beauty. To endure was to be courageous against the devastation that surrounded and engulfed her existence. Sally's story teaches that the courageous person will feel the fear and persevere no matter what the obstacle might be, because as Franklin Roosevelt stated, *'the only thing we have to fear is fear itself.'*

Highlights from Sarah's Story.

- Reaching the point of beauty is not easy particularly if you are battling with a mental health problem
- Look for patterns of unhealthy thoughts and seek help
- Sing uplifting songs, listen to music that uplifts and read uplifting passages from the Bible. The book of Psalms offers many examples of how to overcome feelings of despair
- Look for the lighthouse and focus on the light that gives you direction
- Implement lifestyle changes to combat the pressure-cooker syndrome
- Look for a positive focus such as an existing hobby that gave you a sense of purpose, joy and fulfilment before the onset of your illness
- Do whatever you can to build a healthy body and a healthy mind
- Get out into the fresh air and walk initially for short distances, then increase this activity until it becomes part of your routine
- Look for changes in the way you are thinking and celebrate them
- Give thanks and record your victories in a gratitude journal.

Food for Thought

Use the space below to record the following:

1) One thing that you are grateful for and how it makes you feel good about yourself.
2) Your creative skills and how you can use them to become stronger?

CHAPTER FOUR

Flames of Discouragement: The Quest for Courage

But as for you, ye thought evil against me; but God meant it unto good, to bring to pass, as it is this day, to save much people alive.

Genesis 50:20

It is a natural part of life to feel discouraged from time to time. These are times when we lose confidence and lose the zest and enthusiasm we had for life. The discouragement might come from how others criticise or misuse us. It might be due to a lack of self-confidence or a feeling of being under-valued. It could equally be due to low self-esteem. What we already know, about ourselves and our performance, can disappear as we listen to what others say about us. The things that gave us a sense of achievement disappear and, in its place, enters negative feelings of fear and self-doubt.

For most people an episode of discouragement passes, and we recover, pick up the pieces and start to reorder our lives. The balance we had is re-established and although we might not forget we nevertheless move on. What we do to contain the discouragement is similar to resetting a dial to give another chance for change to occur. I have heard it said that to reset the dial is similar to removing a dying plant from a pot and replanting it in good soil. This action encourages the plant to recover and grow. Discouragement is like a fire, but if it is kept under control the flames will die down and any damage will be minimised. If, however, the flame is out of control it will progress to the stage when help is needed to limit the damage. During times of discouragement, we can ask if there is a more sinister reason for how we are feeling, and if so, what we can do to calibrate the feelings that inevitably allow a negative mindset to persist.

I like the story of Joseph which is found in the first book of the Bible, Genesis. Joseph was loved and encouraged by his father Jacob to see himself as a great man and a promise of deliverance. He was even given a distinctive coat of many colours which set him apart from his brothers. Unsurprisingly, Jacob's actions made his brothers furious, consequently, they plotted to kill him. His brothers threw him into a pit and left him for dead. Joseph was rescued and taken to Egypt and there he faced discouragement. His trajectory changed when he was exalted during a famine when God used him to save his family and his people. He recognised that what his brothers intended for evil, God allowed to turn out for good. Discouragement was transmuted to encouragement.

The next story is a powerful example of how Jamila got up and fought back against the discouragement she encountered as her confidence was stripped away by racism, and the oppressive acts of others.

Jamila's Journey

I wouldn't say that I shouldn't have taken my degree, but over the years I came back to my first love, and it gave me an outlet, it brought healing in a way that I could express myself creatively. This is where my heart is, because every opportunity I get I am doing something creative.

Jamila revealed that she had her ashes experience after losing her job. She was raised in a Christian family and believed that, as it states in Romans 8:28:

All things work together for good to them that love God, to them that are called according to his purpose.

Romans 8:28

Although at the time Jamila did not want to admit it, she now admits that she was a victim of racism. She was successful in her career but wanted to take a leap of faith which led her outside the comfort zone she enjoyed. This leap of faith was not because she felt that it was something that was gifted to her, neither was it a profession for which she was qualified or one where her parents had the skill and passed it onto her, but it was a career choice she wanted to explore. She specified, *'I had been confident with using my right brain.'* She had always thought of herself as a creative person but wanted to challenge herself and move in a new direction. She stated:

> *It is okay when you are performing well but when you step outside your comfort zone and into another job, it is not the same.*

Her first leap of faith came when she decided to emigrate to the United States of America and initially settled in New York. She found a job that gave her satisfaction and where she was happy. Jamila was fortunate to have a caring and helpful manager and with his encouragement, she completed a business degree and was set for life on the high seas of achievement.

After completing the four-year degree, she felt ready to set out on her journey, but her testing was to come after she secured her first position as an auditor. It was one of those moments when she felt good about herself. She said:

> *It felt good, I was confident, and that is what I was all about, developing myself.*

Gaining her first job exceeded her expectations but little did she know that her expectations were soon to be ruined. The organisation where she was employed had no black staff and she had become part of a quota system to prove that they wanted to employ black people. Managers and fellow colleagues did not like the fact that she had been offered a job to become a part of their team and undermined her. She was frozen out and ignored. During the early stages of her employment, she encountered poor treatment, hostility, bullying and denial of support. As a result, she failed to make her mark. Reflecting on this experience she said:

> *It was a set-up because they knew that if they didn't give me support, I would fail.*

She continued:

> *After I lost my job, I took a nosedive and I went into depression which involved me blaming myself, but I did not see it as racism.*

She questioned herself, second-guessing herself and saying inwardly, *Why did you do this? You know you could not do it.* In the midst of self-doubt, Jamila felt as if she was about to lose her faith, but she decided that her focus should not be on the people in the team but on God. She said:

It was because I did not want to get to a point where I lost my faith.

Asked what helped her to make it through the dark days, Jamila said her family was a key source of support. She commented:

There were others that supported and helped me to get back on my feet, but I was not confident in asking for help, instead I was in denial.

At one time, she was at the point of going to meet someone who could help and 'ducked out of it.' She said:

I had voices coming at me saying that if I sued the church, I would be taking money away from old people and they made me sign something to say that I would not sue them for racial discrimination.

At this point Jamila became tearful as she recalled her experience of racism and bullying. It was a flame that was still burning.

The Quest to Find Beauty

Jamila rose out of the ashes when she got a job in an organisation where she was not judged by the colour of her skin. She stated:

I was working in an environment with people who looked like me, they were black.

She was given support and with time was able to develop 'self-confidence and self-respect to recover because of feelings of inadequacy, self-blame and feeling bad about myself.' Gaining the courage to move in a new direction determined the outcome of her journey. Courage is when we are able to move outside of our comfort zone and search for new opportunities even as the dark clouds hover.

As Jamila reflected on this experience, she was reminded that in her youth her intended career was to become a fashion designer. She had hidden her talent, opting for a course that she thought would bring financial rewards. She said:

The minute I showed people pictures of my work, they said what are you doing here?

The most helpful strategies for Jamila were to take the initiative to reach out, reclaim her faith to believe that God can do all things, believing that He is in control. This mindset eventually gave her the ability to be courageous, to reach out to family and friends asking for help. Although she wanted to return home and be surrounded by family, she avoided this action, preferring to think of ways in which she could restructure her life. Her first love was fashion, it was a career she had initially chosen but was side-tracked. On the days when she felt overwhelmed Jamila spent time in fabric shops. She changed her focus and began to design shawls and clothing. She was happy to begin crocheting and knitting even when she was watching television; it seemed to transport her to another realm. Reclaiming her mind promoted emotional and mental wellness.

Jamila exchanged ashes for beauty after she made a conscious decision to gain mastery over her mind, making time for self-care physically and emotionally. She finds pleasure in massage, looking after her body by regularly exercising, and singing, all of which helps her to feel a sense of self-worth. She pointed to a book that gave her considerable insight during a time of discouragement. It was a publication by the late Stephen Covey. His book, called "The 7 Habits of Highly Effective People", made a significant impact on her thinking power. It was the writings of Covey that pushed her in a new direction to become organised and to 'start with the end in mind.' She took his advice and began writing a gratitude journal each day. It was this insight that led her on a new path. In developing spiritual awareness, she regularly listens to good sermons, meditates and studies the Bible, where she gathers gems for everyday situations.

Reflecting on Jamila's Journey: Healing by Choice

Jamila chose to heal because she needed to stop feeling that what had happened was her fault. She exchanged her ashes experience for confidence by restoring and reclaiming her creative brain. Her biggest loss was the feeling of inadequacy, and her greatest gain was becoming assertive, allowing herself to cry and being able to challenge situations that called for change. She said:

That is something beautiful because I emerged out of it and I am now in a position where I train new staff, I do course writing. I can provide the type of support that I did not have. I will always remember how I felt because people left me to struggle, but out of it, God has given me the ability to stand up for my rights.

The passage of scripture that Jamila wants to share with others who are going through a similar experience is:

Fear not, for I am with you; be not dismayed, for I am your God;
I will strengthen you, I will help you, I will uphold you with my
righteous right hand.

Isaiah 41:10

Support: Jamila's comments showed that support is very important during an ashes experience because it helps us to form a spiritual connection with God and with others. It is the lack of support that forces a person to feel depressed which ushers in unwanted feelings of abandonment, loneliness and helplessness. On the other hand, when there are people who are willing to give support, it breaks the isolation by giving us the opportunity to share our experiences.

The concept of social support has been given attention in the research literature showing that it is a person's perception or experience of being loved, nurtured and cared for by others. Support can be given in many ways, it involves nurturance, warmth, food, financial assistance, friendship and a sense of social integration within a network of people who act as a safety net.

The concept of interconnectedness is when a person feels a sense of connection to others since at a cosmological level nothing is disconnected, people are centrally connected and provide help during times of storms that bring testing of the most severe kind. As we progress through each narrative, you will notice that support makes all the difference to survival and resilience because it relieves psychological distress and contributes to recovery.

Reclaiming and Rebuilding

The act of reclaiming is an important strategy for constructing one's personal ability to become courageous. It reinforces the need to believe in one's ability to overcome. Jamila recognised that she had inner resources that, for whatever reason, she had set aside in preference for another pathway. However, she was met with racism which took away her confidence and made her feel insignificant. Finding the path to her true passion meant reframing her life. It called for a bold step, moving away from an environment that was destructive and soul-destroying. This action is similar to having a picture in a broken frame. Reframing the picture helps us to see the world through different lenses. Reframing puts us in the driving seat so that we can turn defeat into triumph, in order to create a link between faith, hope and survival. We can reframe and rebuild our lives after negative experiences, as a result of the choices we make. We do this not in our own strength but in God's strength and according to the purpose He gives us to move in a new direction.

Thinking of this concept of reframing, the life of John Newton ably demonstrates this point. Newton's mother, died when he was six years old and his father quickly remarried. From that point forward he was neglected, and his behaviour became uncontrollable. He had no respect for himself or others. His father sent him to boarding school and then to sea. Newton made his first voyage at eleven years and became the master of slave ships. He was morally bankrupt and referred to himself as an infidel. He became known for his attempts to commit murder and even to commit suicide.

There were storms that almost took his life, but he was saved. After his encounter with Christ during mid-life he was changed and he wrote many hymns, among them was a hymn called "Amazing Grace". He had moved from being wretched and blind to seeing the light. This hymn came to fame after the lyrics were set to song and was sang by Mahalia Jackson at Civil Rights rallies. It is one of the many well-known hymns he wrote that have come into popular usage. It is said that Newton rose from disgrace to amazing grace. He became influential and a key player in his fight for the abolition of slavery. It was his encouragement to William Wilberforce, a member of Parliament to become a Christian politician that won him fame. His transformation brought change to the world, most notably the abolition of slavery after he wrote a booklet called 'Thoughts upon the African Slave Trade.' In truth, Newton became a prolific writer who dedicated his life to prayer and the doctrine of love.

We are given a second chance to make a conscious choice to transform so that we can rebuild and reframe our lives. These are creative strategies that lead to personal freedom. At the end of his life, he had moved from describing himself as an infidel to a great sinner and Christ as a great Saviour.

> Amazing Grace, how sweet the sound that saved a wretch like me
> I once was lost but now I'm found was blind but now I see.
>
> JOHN NEWTON

Racism and Discrimination

The experiences of racism, discrimination and inequality can lead a person to walk through ashes and go through a storm. It results in a loss of confidence, self-blaming, over-whelm, low self-esteem, loss of identity, disempowerment and inability to think from a position of strength. Researchers have found that racism and discrimination lead to depression and in general adversely affect mental health (Williams et al, 2019). It has a negative impact on all sectors of a person's life. It can reinforce negative stereotypes and prohibit people from attaining the basic necessities that sustain life. In short, it damages self-worth.

It is more difficult to ask for help or accept it when we are at a low point and particularly when there are systemic practices that deny equal opportunities. It was interesting to hear about the strategies that led Jamila to regain her confidence and reduced the negative feelings that eventually led to her own empowerment. The concept of empowerment is a pillar of strength because it releases harmful internal feelings and gives us personal power to achieve our goals and ambitions.

As Steve Maraboli stated, the beauty of life is that you are:

> Put on this earth to achieve your greatest self to live out your purpose and to do it courageously.

It is only with insight that we can reflect on life and see the progress we have made and the distance we have come.

There is a saying that knowledge is power, but this is not true. It is not the knowledge that is power, but it is what we do with the knowledge that is most powerful. Unless we become knowledgeable of the systems that are holding us back, and take action, there will be no change. Simply having the knowledge is not enough to transform us or open the door to healing.

The past is where we store all our memories, both good and bad. We store in our minds the things that our parents, teachers and those in powerful positions have told us or done to us. We come to believe these messages and hold on to them. The words that others pronounce may even stunt our growth. When we need validation of our thinking, the things we have been taught about life are resurrected from the deepest recesses of the unconscious part of our minds. Although it is a difficult process to let go of negativity, it is the only way to find peace. Peace cannot co-exist with a cluttered mind. Insight comes when we develop self-awareness. This is the ability to begin making the changes that are necessary to move along a continuum and the structures that might be holding us back and literally keeping us stuck in a position from which we cannot find liberation.

Courageous people can become like eagles with great vision, looking down and seeing everything that is around and beneath them which includes the target for which they are aiming. The analogy of the eagle allows me to think that if an eagle refuses to learn how to use its wings and stays in a pen with ducklings, it will be impossible for him to empower himself and do what he should be doing, namely soaring. In order to move from ashes to beauty, you must be positive, surround yourself with positive people and become open to self-scrutiny. You must understand the importance of being focused on reaching a stage where you can start being enthusiastic enough to work on specific areas of your life in which you are seeking direction and greater fulfilment. In thinking of the boat and the storm, the tide and the current of the water was against Jamila but her quest for change led her to become a beacon of light and hence, hope. It is important to remember that even though the current might be strong, it is possible to fight against it. God is in the storm of discouragement, and He is the true captain of your boat.

Highlights based on Jamila's Story

- Let go of the past – the past is what will hold you back
- Let go of discouragement – discouragement defeats and will stop you from being productive
- Let go of mental clutter because it does not serve you well
- Find ways to be creative – creativity leads to an organised mind
- Find people you can talk to – share your worries and concerns particularly when it is impacting your health negatively
- Seek support – support alleviates anxiety and self-doubt, helping to build a confident outlook simply by knowing that there is someone who will help in your hour of need
- Refuse to internalise negative valuations – believe in your value and your worth by refuting the lies that others speak about you. Rather listen to the still small voice of God speaking peace to your soul
- Learn how to become assertive and fight for your rights

- Learn how to self-care – spend time relaxing, create time for leisure, diet, exercise, fresh air, and rest
- Turn your heart towards God – He is the only one who can give true healing and restoration of the heart
- Be the eagle – soar to heights that others thought were impossible.

Food for Thought

Choose two of the highlights from Jamila's story and write your personal reflections in the box below.

1) Think back to an action you have taken to overcome an ashes experience in your personal life. What was the outcome for you?
2) What actions can you take when you are feeling discouraged?

CHAPTER FIVE

Opening the Door

> When one door of happiness closes, another one opens, but often, we look so long at the closed door that we do not see the one that has been opened for us.
>
> HELEN KELLER

The story of Helen Keller is a remarkable one because she became both deaf and blind after contracting a childhood disease. A door was opened for Helen after she met a teacher who became instrumental in helping her to recognise words and eventually to speak. The realisation of her inner ability opened many doors of opportunity for her so that she was able to excel despite her lack of speech. She was able to cross the divide between ability and disability.

One of the biggest doors that ever opened for me was when I decided to leave academia and embark on setting up my freelance business. I had no particular understanding of how to set up a business, but I had the leadership skills and the motivation to move in a new direction. When I started to develop my business over thirty years ago, I thought that only people with a background in business management or coming from a wealthy family with a history of business could be leaders. It was not until I started to work with leaders that I discovered that this notion was far from true. There were many struggles and hurdles I had to overcome to allow myself to believe that I could make a living out of working for myself and make it on my own. I had heard the saying that it is not what you know but who you know that allows you to climb the ladder of success. To a greater extent, this is true because some people experience a meteoric rise, they do very little work and yet rise and move through organisations with minimum trouble and maximum ease. Yet, others have to work hard to grow and develop. I was in the second camp.

My ashes experience during my work life came when I was determined to move the boundaries and obstacles that stood in my way. As a black woman, I found it difficult to get through my working day because of the attitudes of others. I was often told that what I was experiencing was not because I was black or a woman but because I was hanging my hat too high. In other words, they considered that my expectations were above what they thought I was capable of achieving.

The lack of support I experienced often led me to feel disillusioned and on my own. I recall driving in my car after visiting a student on placement and hearing a song with the words, "Here I am on my own again." These words resonated with me because it felt like a repeating scene in a play. I had left a job where I was all but discouraged. I was overcome by tears as I listened and sang the song out loud. I knew that it was referring to me, I was that person that was alone even though I was surrounded by people. I had no one within the work setting to talk to or to express how low I was feeling. I felt disempowered. I began to think about how I could escape the prison called work I was going to every day just to make a living. There were days when my colleagues dismissed my suggestions and underrated the contribution I made. I struggled to make sense of what I was doing and often asked myself if I was indeed reaching for an unattainable goal. I discovered that my colleagues were jealous of my teaching style and the respect I was gaining from students. Yet it was a door that was opened for me.

In the early days of my teaching career during 1994, two of my male colleagues asked if I would co-teach with them and I willingly agreed. When we arrived in the classroom, I discovered that they had not done any preparation. To say the least, they were unscrupulous and made their reputation among the students by telling jokes, laughing and making light of serious matters. Integrity was one of the values I upheld, but when I marked papers and students did not achieve the pass grade, I was criticised for not giving a few extra marks to save them having to repeat an assignment. Although I had no evidence for it, it appeared as if my colleagues were unethical in their relationships and boundaries with young and impressionable female students. Thus, some of the students liked them and excused their behaviour as frivolous and as male machismo.

In our planning meeting for the joint teaching session, they said to me, if you find that you are struggling to keep up with us, this is the sign you should look for and we will rescue you. Apparently, it was a technique they used to cover for each other. In like manner, I was given a sign that would resonate with them. Metaphorically speaking it was intended to rescue me from the flames. When we began the teaching session I felt as if I was in deep water and up a creek without a paddle. They did not give the sign and I was left defenceless and felt humiliated in the presence of an entire group of students. I could see that the students were aware that we were not singing from the same song sheet. I began to crumble, and all of my well-thought-out plans went up in smoke as I became nervous and began to shake. I felt embarrassed as the session suddenly took a turn for the worse. I could literally feel my feet wobbling and wanting to give way beneath me. I wished that the ground would open and swallow me up. I could hardly wait for the session to come to an end. I exited the room without collecting my papers or staying behind to talk to students, which is what I usually did. Emotionally, I was a wreck. I did not know that this plan was designed by my colleagues to unsettle me and make me lose my confidence. At the end of the class, I went to my office and closed the door, I bowed my head and prayed for courage to face the students. Before I had opened my eyes, I heard a rap on the door and two students presented themselves. I invited them into my office, and they commiserated with me and said that they found what my colleagues had done was appalling. They gave me the courage to hold my head up and return to work the next day.

I was able to collect myself and regain some semblance of self-respect and when I felt ready, I asked for a meeting with my colleagues to discuss what had happened. They both looked at me as if I was hallucinating. I ended the meeting knowing that I could not trust my colleagues to cover my back. It felt like academic ashes but from that day forward, I was determined to make it on my own. I refused to hide in the shadows because I wanted to stand out, stand up and be counted. I certainly did not want to be forced out of my job as was the case for my predecessor, who I came to understand was a talented black woman but they had worn her down with many challenges and insults until she decided to leave. I wanted to do a good job. It was at that time that I was reminded of the words of Jesus when He said:

> Behold I stand at the door and knock, if any man hears my voice, and opens the door I will come in and eat with him and he with me. To him that overcomes I will give the right to sit with me on my throne just as I overcame and sat down with my father on his throne.
>
> Revelation 3:20

It was as if God was telling me to open up the door to a new reality and a new way of moving forward. I knew that if I allowed him to come in and dine with me, He would give me assurance and reassurance. For the next two years, I consolidated my teaching skills and became well-known for my abilities. Eventually, a decision was made that the college would be closing and the course would be transferred to a university. At this time, I had the choice to leave or to take the transfer. I made the decision to stay, take the transfer with a promotion to senior lecturer but reduce my hours to a part-time member of staff. I used the other half of my time to return to social work practice and was successful in getting a newly created job on a part-time basis with the local authority as a Reviewing Officer.

This role allowed me to gain an insight into the needs of looked-after children and their rights for advocacy and other mandatory services as well as developing leadership skills as a Chair. I was able to blend practice knowledge and transfer this wisdom back to the classroom. The students loved what I brought as I shared examples of poor and good practice. Out of my academic ashes experience I began to plan my phased entry into the world of entrepreneurship. I could see the opportunity to develop course content and was given the vision to create a niche in the market. I had good research and consultation skills, which placed me in a position to create my brand of courses and market services based on my knowledge, expertise and experience.

Moving away from an environment that is toxic can become a lifeline even though it may appear that one is in a position to sink. The boat may not have the correct reinforcement and support to make the journey, therefore strength must be drawn from within. I purposed in my heart to swim even though I would be doing it against the tide. Without vision, I would not have been able to see the beauty. In this storm I was sinking and not knowing how to negotiate a way out of it. It suddenly became clear to me that my best way out was the power of creative thinking and decision-making.

There were several keys in my ashes experiences; the first was the key that opened the door to success. This key was knowing God and extending my trust and faith in Him. This key requires consistent prayer, but it also requires a period of waiting to see God's plan unfold. The second key was self-belief. This meant trusting my inner feelings and not being overcome by negative emotions, but at the same time noticing the pitfalls, patterns and problems. The pitfalls represent the traps that others set for you, the patterns are the way you respond. The problems are the situations that need to be solved.

The third key was knowing self. This key was associated with my identity and believing that I had the capabilities to become a good lecturer. In the work environment I was a black woman working in a white- and male-dominated environment. This brought its own challenges because it made the water even more treacherous, turbulent and unpredictable. The fourth key was to remember that when God opens a door no one can close it. These were my keys to freedom.

Keys to Freedom

> For you were called to freedom, brothers. Only do not use your freedom as an opportunity for the flesh, but through love serve one another.
>
> Galatians 5:13

Freedom comes from the way we think and how we use it as an opportunity to serve others. Even when we are in a position of power and authority, we must nevertheless use the position we are in to improve outcomes for those who are in a less favourable position than ourselves. Freedom comes through a strong foundation of faith in God's ability to carry us through the rough storms of life and find the strength to survive. We must use the key of freedom to think from a position of strength. Instead of believing what others tell us we must give ourselves permission to believe in our own potential and capabilities. Too often we are waiting for others to validate and tell us that we are good enough when in actuality what we need is to be able to say it to ourselves.

Freedom is to know that you know what you know. Far too often we engage in doubt, particularly when we feel that we are lacking in skills and knowledge. In order to know, you must be willing to learn and to put yourself out to create change in your life. No matter how helpful people might be they are unable to tell us what we know because knowing originates from within. When you know what you know you will use your personal power to repeat it to yourself. Convince yourself that you know it. The word of God says:

> Study to show thyself approved unto God, a workman that needeth not to be ashamed, rightly dividing the word of truth.
>
> 2 Timothy 2:15

When I embarked on my PhD studies, I felt like a fish out of water. I looked at other students and had the tendency to think that I could not match up to them. I had very little support from my supervisor, but I had heard the call to study. I made sacrifices that were unheard of. While setting up and getting my consultancy business off the ground I was working part-time and studying at a higher level without the correct support. Yet, against the odds, I persevered and reached my dream. Life is not plain sailing because, in this example, I had a lecturer who was disinterested in my success. She spent my supervision sessions talking incessantly about herself and her accomplishments. Then one day God removed her and the obstacles she was placing in my way disappeared and I was given the freedom to move forward unafraid.

Recently, I was offered the opportunity to become a TED speaker. I chose to speak about how I became a resilient black woman. As I was rehearsing my speech, I knew what I wanted to say, but at times I was afraid that I would forget the words, therefore, I told myself that I knew it. Minutes before walking onto the stage I went to the bathroom and prayed to be imbued with the Holy Spirit. I was confident and gave one of the best speeches I have ever given. The freedom to speak came not only from the realisation that all things are possible but also knowing that God would bring back each word, each sentence, and each paragraph to my memory. Jesus encouraged us to know that:

> With men this is impossible, but with God all things are possible.
>
> Matthew 19:26

There is a significant difference between people who are positive and negative. Positive people strive to overcome hurdles while negative people constantly complain and fail to take personal responsibility. George Washington Carver stated that *'ninety-nine percent of all failures come from people who have a habit of making excuses.'* This is a valid point if you think that people fail to reach their point of beauty because they do not realise that even in the darkest hour there is freedom to act from a position of power.

Freedom of thought gives us the willingness to go out on a limb because that is often where the low-lying fruit is waiting to be picked. People who stay in their comfort zone will never experience the freedom to do something that is unique and different from what other people are doing. It means using every opportunity as a stepping stone to better things and as a path to success.

Gaining the victory over self-doubt came as a result of taking action. I began to fight back when I felt powerless and as if there was no rudder beneath my boat during the storm or hiding place as I went through the ashes. I tested out my sails and I reached for the anchor, which was Jesus. The chorus of a song I knew from childhood was repeated over and over again. This chorus was:

"My hope is built on nothing less
Than Jesus' blood and righteousness.
I dare not trust the sweetest frame,
But wholly lean on Jesus' name."
Chorus:
"On Christ the solid Rock, I stand;
All other ground is sinking sand,
All other ground is sinking sand."

This hymn was written by Edward Mote. He carried the lyrics in his pocket. As he was visiting the sick wife of a friend who was near the point of dying; he reached into his pocket and presented it to those around her bedside. It is the only hymn he ever wrote, but it came to great fame as many people realised that it was a victorious hymn. It was his spirit of audacity that gave him the courage to write a song that has over the years brought courage to many facing despair and disappointment. The spirit of audacity allowed me to stand on solid rock which was the word of God. There have been many turbulent storms in my life, nevertheless I responded to them by holding fast to Christian values, among them are gratitude, endurance and perseverance.

Highlights From My Personal Story

- It takes courage to stand up for your beliefs
- Do not be afraid to move out of your comfort zone
- When you are facing a problem and feel as if you are ship-wrecked look for the master of the storm, the one who can bring calm and peace into your life

- Look for the beauty in the ashes and you will find something that is burning in the embers
- Look for doors of opportunity and use them to your advantage
- Be proactive during the times when one door closes; look for the one that opens
- Do not be discouraged by other people's negative comments and judgments
- Choose to think from the perspective of freedom.

Food for Thought

Write a personal experience in the box below that felt like ashes for you. As you reflect remember that disappointment can make or break you.

1) What did disappointment do to you?
2) Describe the actions you took to create positive change and turn it into a beautiful outcome.
3) Recall and record how it led to freedom.

In the next story, there is an apt example of how ashes turned into beauty as Davina used the concept of freedom to take the first step to reach her goal.

Davina's Journey: The Quest for a New Direction

I was a healthy person but, as I hit my 30s, I had many health problems and God could have taken my life, so the beauty is that I lived.

Davina's ashes experience happened when she was working in New York as a nurse. She had gained a master's degree in nursing and was looking for a new opportunity. She spoke thus:

I applied for the position of assistant head nurse, but the position was given to another person, and she didn't even have a bachelor's degree.

Shortly after this disappointment, Davina was visiting California and, on her way back home, she fell and broke her toe as she was alighting from a bus. It was a fracture that took her on a journey of physical pain. On a previous visit to California, she had seen a university and thought that she would like the opportunity to work there. She shared her dream with a friend but did not receive a positive response. It took several months for Davina's toe to heal, but while she was recuperating, she decided to call the university to see if there was a vacant position to become a member of the nursing faculty. As it turned out there was a vacant position to teach in her area of nursing. Immediately Davina applied, she was interviewed on the phone and was offered the position. She said:

I would consider that to be moving from ashes to beauty, the pain was not only physical but emotional because I was turned down for a position for which I was over-qualified.

Although Davina had no particular plan to complete a PhD it was an opportunity that came while she was thinking of what her next step should be. She commented:

I had no plan to do a doctorate; it was not on my radar screen. Every year I had to reapply for my position as a lecturer, but the chairperson said to me, if you plan to stay in academia, you should do a PhD.
One day I received a flyer about an opportunity to attend a seminar,

discussing doctoral studies. I immediately decided to attend that seminar. When I got there, I met a representative from the university who was an African American woman. I discovered that it was a recruitment seminar. I applied and was accepted to start my doctoral studies. When I started, she took me under her wing and mentored me. Incidentally, when I finished my studies, she resigned. I am sure she did not plan it that way, but it was as if God had opened that door for me.

One of Davina's strategies was to consider other opportunities. She stated:

I knew that I loved teaching, so I used my experience to look for other ways to move on. I am the type of person who is very persistent. If I am told that I can't do something I will go to all lengths to do it because I am very persistent.

In exploring her Christian values, Davina said:

I have been a Christian for a long time, there were verses that came to me, such as trust the Lord with all your heart and lean not onto your own understanding, in all your ways acknowledge Him and He will direct your paths (Proverbs 3:5-6).

It was a verse her mother had given to her as a young person, and it stayed with her throughout her life. *She stated:*

I trusted in the Lord, the strength came from God, the support came from family and friends, and I moved on.

Moving on from the ashes is what helped Davina because for her it was an innate belief in her abilities. She said: you have to believe in yourself. What appeared to be a disappointment and a loss became a stepping stone because her sphere of contact and influence grew in a way that she did not anticipate.

Believe that you won't let others get in your way, and believe that no one will stop you, you are not going to give up and not let others stop you.

As a result of her fearless spirit Davina became successful in her career. In later life Davina was able to enjoy memories of friendships, of helping numerous students to qualify as nurses, and she recalls travelling to many destinations. Many years later she was able to make the transition during retirement and is now living in a community home for senior citizens where she continues to use her skills to help others. She has found herself in the company of ex-professionals where she continues to share her knowledge. Davina continues to read and study, both of which she declares has given her "freedom". She has the time to reflect on her life, the places she has visited, the people she met and the contribution she has made to the lives of others.

Reflecting on Davina's experience

Davina's experience emphasised several key concepts that a person must practise to emerge out of ashes.

Making a Transition: Moving on is an important step in making a transition since it encourages a process of change to begin. After a disappointment people must learn how to move on without regret, hard feelings or resentment. It takes resilience to be able to move when it feels as if you are immobilised and stuck in one position. Physical strength is required to move and reach a milestone, but it also requires a high level of motivation and self-determination to move emotionally and psychologically. Davina's decision to move on involved making significant adjustments such as physically moving to a new location, giving up her home, making new friends, adjusting to a new job, learning new skills and taking the opportunity to engage in advanced studies.

Moving on is a transition, and all transitions involve endings and new beginnings, they also involve change that can, if we allow them, result in beauty. Preparation is required to accommodate change, part of which is about making new attachments by building and sustaining new relationships. I found each of these factors in Davina's experience, which began with being overlooked for promotion but which led to an unplanned transition and eventually to a crown of beauty.

Transitions are difficult, particularly when they are associated with adversity. It is possible to become stuck in one position, refusing to acknowledge the need to make a new start. Transitions can be determined by the loss of a job or denial of an opportunity which provokes the need for change. The concept of ashes applies to transitions because it relates to loss.

During the time of loss and grief there is a need for others to be empathic by listening and giving support. Davina had support based on family and inner resources as well as her religious beliefs. It is this circle of support that allows a person to make a successful transition, thus moving away from the ashes and toward beauty. As Davina advanced in years, she was able to make one of the most difficult transitions, that of moving from her home to a group home facility where she continued to engage in a supportive role among fellow residents. She continued to read and to study which brought a source of satisfaction contentment and peace. It was her mind-set that made the difference to the person she eventually became.

Acceptance: Davina's narrative demonstrates that acceptance is not equated with giving up, on the contrary, it shows a person's willingness to view life from a position of strength. In order to move on, one must first accept the way things are, nothing can change the ashes, but you can change the way you think about the ashes. This means reaching a stage of acceptance through a strong belief system, that propels and braces up one's "innate ability". She states:

> It is an innate belief in your abilities, the belief in yourself that you won't let others get in your way and that no one will stop you.

Acceptance brings resolution of a problem so that a person is able to put the past behind and move forward. For example, the man in the woods setting a flame to draw attention for rescue, might need to acknowledge that the flame might not be noticed initially. By embracing acceptance, he can foster a mind-set that encourages him to strategise for a more visible signal, ultimately increasing his chances of being rescued. Metaphorically speaking, the woods represent a challenging situation akin to ashes that results from a past ordeal. The act of setting the flames symbolises the resilience to transform adversity into something that is noticeable, much like the beauty that emerges from ashes. The emergence of beauty inevitably comes as a result of the challenges he faces in the woods and how he is able to problem-solve and find a workable solution.

Serenity: The spirit of serenity during times of upheaval and uncertainty is crucial, because it brings a sense of inner peace. This does not mean giving up, but that one recognises the limitations of fighting a battle they cannot win. Reinhold Niebuhr's prayer of serenity states we need to ask God to "grant us serenity to accept the things we cannot change, the courage to change the things we can and the wisdom to know the difference." Serenity allows us to be at peace with the decisions and choices we make. Serenity is a transformative process which involves letting go, in order to find beauty. It is the act of letting go that creates space for new growth, new thoughts and different outcomes. Serenity is a conscious choice to move beyond the ashes to a more hopeful future. Maintaining unwavering trust in God's providence is critical for survival, even in the darkest hours when hope seems lost and after you have lost everything. God has the power to transform the storm and turn ashes into beauty.

Highlights Based on Davina's Story

- Trust in God and believe in yourself
- Do not allow others to pull you down or shatter your dreams
- When you invite God into the boat it stays afloat
- Think who am I? I am a person of worth
- Follow your path and your purpose, do not be put off or side-tracked
- Develop conviction and be convinced of what you know
- Remain focused on your goal by making the most of opportunities that come your way
- Ask God to reveal your calling
- Be of service to others
- Create a picture in your mind of possibilities

- Rise to the challenge
- Open the door to new possibilities.

Food for Thought

Use the box below to reflect on and record the answer to the following questions.

1) Identify two difficult transitions that you had to negotiate, what helped you to move on?
2) How could being serene change your outlook?
3) What was the quality of support you received during your time of a transitional period?

CHAPTER SIX

The Joy and Pain of Relationships

How desperately we want to maintain trust in those we love! In the face of everything, we try to find reasons to trust. Because losing faith is worse than falling out of love.

AUTHOR UNKNOWN

From the day we are born until the day we die, the reality is that we need relationships to survive, we need to be loved, we need to be able to trust and we need those who are closest to us to meet our needs. Babies cannot thrive unless they are fed and given the care they need to survive. No man is an island; therefore, we cannot survive without others to make us complete.

From conception a baby begins a wonderful experience of bonding with their mother in the womb, where they are sustained by the umbilical cord. The amniotic fluid in the womb feeds the baby and allows it to float around and provides a protective environment. After birth the umbilical cord is severed and from that moment forward the baby must learn how to breathe for him/herself. Fathers play an important role in terms of the supportive relationship they have with the mother of their child/ren and after birth the connection they form with the child becomes integral to their growth and development. Attachment relationships begin from childhood and endure through time and space. Nevertheless, relationships between children and their parents can break down and sever, sometimes without reconciliation. The more committed parents are, the more likely it is that they will provide a nurturing, warm and stable environment for their children. Under these conditions children are able to reach their full potential.

As adults we must transact positive and enduring relationships with our partners, our children, and colleagues in different working environments, as well as with people from all walks of life in the communities and neighbourhoods where we live. The ability to develop positive relationships depends by and large on the type of relationships we have had with our parents and significant others during childhood.

Relationships do not materialise overnight; it takes time to get to know people, to trust them and to get along harmoniously with them. While relationships bring pleasure and joy, they also bring considerable pain and heartache. We are often divided and conflicted when relationships go wrong because our emotions are negatively impacted.

For five decades, I resided alongside my neighbours, Roger and Sarah. Both were dedicated educators who left an indelible mark on the education of numerous children, including their own. In their later years, I witnessed the couple's gradual decline, but as they took short walks Sarah carried a walking cane and Roger supported her with his arm. Theirs was a long, committed and fruitful relationship. I was fortunate to be one of the people they gravitated towards. I spent time in their home talking to them and discovered the secret of their close relationship. It was love.

As Sarah declined physically, she retained her mental faculties. However, Roger declined in his mental abilities. Yet, he continued to care for Sarah. He remained active in the house and maintained the garden that bloomed each year with plants and flowers. He created an immaculate garden for Sarah to enjoy as she sat in her favourite chair. In their mid-nineties they passed away in quick succession of each other, leaving behind a once meticulously tended garden, now reclaimed by nature. As people celebrated their enduring union, the prevailing memories were of how things used to be. Their beauty was remembered not as frail and aged, but as a couple with a radiant glow that was the essence of kindness and generosity, a testament to the way they lived and their enduring relationship.

Marriage is intended to be a lifelong union between two individuals, granted to some like Roger and Sarah who had the privilege of remaining together until death. Yet others encounter problems leading to separation and divorce. For a number of unforeseen reasons people stop loving and caring for each other. The love that attracted them to each other may disappear. Within fractured relationships is the reminder that shared lives can unveil a difficult and turbulent journey. In the next narrative Maranda is forced to find her way out of the ashes of a broken marriage.

Maranda's Story: Ashes from a Broken Marriage

I had lost my marriage and my friends, I had given up my job, I had lost my home, and I was financially abused. I couldn't find a permanent job. I felt that everything had gone to cinders. There was no support for me and the children. There was no future for me and the children. I could not see a future beyond what was going on.

Maranda's narrative unfolds as a poignant account of a marriage that disintegrated, marked by themes of unfaithfulness, brokenness, the loss of her home and financial abuse. Maranda's fifteen-year marriage came to an end when her husband decided that he wanted the family to return to their country of birth. Sensing that her marriage was near the point of disintegration, Maranda agreed to relocate to their homeland with their two children. She made this joint decision with her husband, believing that the change would inject new life and vigour into their marriage. Having resigned from her job, sold the family home and uprooted their children, Maranda and Bob set out for a new life. However, this dream quickly crumbled, and the relationship deteriorated soon after their arrival. Uprooted from her familiar environment, family and support systems, Maranda found herself in an environment where she had no family or friends to whom she could reach out to for support. The funds they had received after selling their home was secured in a bank account by her husband to which she had no access. Furniture from their home began to disappear without her consent.

Bob's close relationship with his siblings intensified her loss and isolation and while supporting his close family network she was denied support. Maranda felt a sense of abandonment and had no power to change her circumstances. She began to lose weight and her health deteriorated. She said, *'I think that was when I first developed diabetes.'*

Maranda found it difficult to secure a permanent job exacerbated by her situation, her financial instability added to her stress-induced insolation and fear of what would happen to herself and her children. It was a situation that left her pondering over an uncertain future. Maranda confessed that:

It felt like ashes because if you think about ashes, you think about everything being burnt and nothing is left, it was like cinders, and everything was lost because everything began to crumble.

In addition, Maranda was left rudderless; there were no sails to chart her course and no lighthouse on the distant horizon. The future appeared bleak because she was totally reliant on a man who did not love her and whose rejection she acutely felt. She concluded, *'It meant nothing to him.'* She had no outlet, and the stakes of her marriage surviving were low. Her choices were to find a way to leave a loveless marriage or stay and endure the emotional pain of rejection. The pain of betrayal, abandonment, and deceit took a toll on Maranda's emotional and physical wellbeing. Sleepless nights, stress, and weight loss were marked by a period of deep suffering.

At her lowest point Maranda was forced into a position where she had to initiate divorce proceedings, which led to further emotional turmoil and strain. The end of her marriage brought finality to a relationship that she had thought would last for a lifetime. Despite the hope that her husband would rekindle the relationship, it was a hope that did not materialise. It was at this point that Maranda recognised the need to move on and take positive steps to secure her own and her children's future. After fifteen years of marriage, she was left desolate and as if she had nothing to show for the investment she had made in the relationship with her husband. Maranda declared:

It was a traumatic time, but God stepped in and allowed me to return home to my family in England and be with my family where I felt safe.

I wasn't eating, the weight fell off. I was constantly in physical and emotional pain.

Finding herself in an intolerable situation, Maranda made the decision to be reunited with her mother and siblings. Her struggle did not end, and the ashes continued to burn. She was forced to care for her children single-handedly and without any financial support from their father. She stated that over and above everything it was his unfaithfulness that became her biggest loss.

It was many years before Maranda could accept that her marriage had ended. Becoming a single parent with all the responsibility resting on her shoulders was a difficult experience, because she had to find employment, accommodation, and settle her children into new schools. There were turbulent years, but she states, God always provided a job. She said:

I could see how God provided for me in immeasurable ways to turn the bad into something good.

She likened divorce to a death, the only difference being that with a deceased person you can go to the grave and leave flowers.

It was Maranda's acceptance that created her journey towards independence and new opportunities. Discovering her gift for writing, she authored more than one book of poems that she had accumulated over many years. Her quest for beauty came when she found the strength in writing poems that gave her an emotional outlet. This was the essence of her transformation, and it eventually became her lighthouse. Among her achievements were gaining a business degree and gaining continuous employment.

Reflecting on Maranda's Journey: New Opportunities

One of the luxuries we do not have in life is perfect relationships, because we live in an imperfect world. We all experience struggles and difficulties that are perplexing, some are more entrenched and difficult to solve than others. Under conditions of stress, disagreement and conflict, relationships can become brittle, they can fracture and even sever, sometimes to the point of no return and where connections cease to exist. Relationships can break down between couples, parents and children, between siblings, cousins, uncles and aunts. In a marriage the couple may fail to see or accept the pain they are causing. They may become spiteful and vengeful in an attempt to prove a point or gain leverage. They can also do harm as they seek to influence others by maligning a person's character and by engaging in blaming and other disempowering tactics.

After a person has had an experience of a broken relationship, they may lose trust, feel vulnerable and rejected. It might not only be the opposite sex, but they may lose trust with people in general. It is usually the fear of being hurt again that makes them suspicious of people's motives. They may blame themselves in the aftermath of the dissolution of a relationship, particularly if they had hope of what is stated in the Bible, "until death do us part" because marriage is seen as a union and a long-term commitment, the hope is that it will last. Even though relationships may break down, if there is the will to take personal responsibility it can change a hopeless situation into a hopeful one as long as there is support, and as the song by Bette Midler suggests, one partner becomes the support or the "wind beneath my wings."

Maranda's narrative clearly identifies an experience that felt like ashes. It was for her a time when everything was burnt and nothing was left, everything was lost, and her life began to crumble. She emphasised feeling the sting of rejection. She recalled that her experience led to loss and disillusionment. Maranda said:

I did not have a job or a place to call home, it was like everything was stripped away from me. It made me feel like there was no future.

One of the most difficult emotions to cope with is that of rejection. In the maze of life, we often find ourselves grappling with the harsh realities of being unloved, uncared for and being unappreciated. Feelings of rejection can leave us battered and bruised, similar to a ship in a violent storm, and its sting can cast a dark shadow over our self-worth, opening the door to negative thoughts and disillusionment. We may even feel undeserving of love, and it can haunt us to the point of feeling paralysed. In the swirling feelings of nothingness, we can lose sight of the expectations we had as they seemingly recede into the background.

Rejection has a way of wrapping us in a cocoon of self-doubt, making it difficult to see beyond the pain that is associated with ashes. In a real sense we lose sight of our aspirations, hopes and dreams, replacing them with fear.

Overcoming rejection is an enormous task at a time when the feeling of disappointment looms large. Nevertheless, it is a task that requires courage to take small steps that will move us in the direction of healing and recovery. Each step you take must be determined in order for a new-found strength to emerge and take the place of the sadness and agony that became a threat to your survival. You may recall that I talked about the importance of an anchor; it applies when you are feeling rejected and as if you are on shifting sand without a grip to hold you firmly to the rock. The reality is that you have lost a person from your life, but you have not lost everything. It is the anchor that attaches to the solid rock and gives the boat something to hold on to. The solid rock is Jesus.

As I reflected on Maranda's journey and how life changed for her, it was her hope and faith that became strong pillars of her strength. She embraced the belief that even ashes could be turned into beauty. It was the way she transmuted the disappointment she felt into opportunities that became her saving grace. Drawing parallels with Biblical verses she used them to strengthen her resolve to win the battle. She attributed the end of a marriage as the beginning a newfound independence, strength and purpose. In no small way, Maranda's narrative demonstrates the potential for growth and new opportunities after the ending of a relationship. Through faith, trust, and embracing independence, she not only overcame the ashes but through the process, also discovered her latent and hitherto undiscovered talents and gifts.

Maranda's journey exemplifies the profound transformation that is possible when we think of moving from ashes to beauty. Despite the initial devastation of the loss of a relationship she believed would last, it was her unwavering wish to rebuild her life, even under the most challenging circumstances, that turned her life around. In sharing her story, Maranda shows how it is possible to navigate the complexities of separation and loss. She proves that even in the darkest of times, beauty is just beneath the surface.

Hope is the feeling of expectation and desire for something to happen through prayer and believing that God will provide when we are at rock bottom. He gives us his grace and the ability to believe that ashes can be turned into beauty, hope is believing that things will work out in the end. She confidently stated:

> If God can turn night into day, He can turn ashes into beauty, it is an invincible circle. Faith holds on to hope, it turns sadness into gladness, weakness into strength and ashes into beauty.

For Maranda it was her prayer life and faith journey that counteracted her negative experience of loss into the assurance that God would provide for her needs. Her quest for beauty came as she took steps to change her script and become independent. It also came through her determination to proactively seek change and as Paul the Apostle expresses it: press towards the mark of a higher calling.

> Brethren, I count not myself to have apprehended: but this one thing I do, forgetting those things which are behind, and reaching forth unto those things which are before, I press toward the mark for the prize of the high calling of God in Christ Jesus.
>
> Philippians 3:13-14

Highlights from Maranda's Story

- Remember that ashes may come in many different forms and guises that try to destroy your inner peace, but God wants to give you the oil of gladness
- God is able to restore everything that you have lost
- Be on the lookout for your gifts and work hard to fulfil your potential and God-given abilities
- After a broken relationship look for ways to rebuild your life by focusing on your inner strength and work to improve yourself
- Be hopeful and do not give in to feelings of rejection, fear or low self-worth
- When a love relationship ends avoid self-blame
- Be hopeful and trust God to help you to build new and trusting relationships.

Food for Thought

Use your journal or the box below to write a sentence about the following:

1) How have you coped with a broken relationship?
2) What steps did you take to aid your recovery?
3) What tips would you share with other women going through a similar experience as Maranda?

CHAPTER SEVEN
Overcoming Fear

> I have learned that courage is not the absence of fear but triumph over it. The brave man is not he who does not feel afraid, but he who conquers that fear.
>
> NELSON MANDELA

During times of fire or storm, it is natural to become fearful. Both can lead to destruction, but both require courage. Fear is one of the most destructive emotions we encounter, and many people sink beneath its crushing weight and the grip that it has over them. Fear leads to a lack of confidence and self-efficacy, but it is part of what happens as we are going through the ashes. What we underestimate during times of fear is our own strength to conquer it.

It is interesting that Nelson Mandela, who had spent many years in a South African prison on Robin Island, isolated and alone from family, friends and community, was able to say that it is not the fear that is as important as the ability to rise above it. The deciding factor is our inner conviction that leads to the actions we take to master and subdue fear. In his speech "I am the First Accused", Mandela declared that fear should not be allowed to stand in the way of progress. He knew that if the people of South Africa were unable to be fearless and courageous, it would be impossible for them to create a new democracy. The same was true for President de Gaulle as he fled in fear from the Germans who threatened to overthrow France. President de Gaulle's focus was on liberation and hope. He firmly asked the question, 'Must we abandon all hope? Is our defeat final?' His answer was an emphatic No! Fear and freedom are inextricably linked, since it is impossible to be truly free and liberated unless we are able to challenge the fear that threatens and challenges us to be brave and stand in the hope that we can escape its grip.

Fear is a part of who we are, we learn from children how to respond to the challenges we meet on a daily basis. When bullied, some children will stand up and fight, but others will run away or succumb to their attackers. As adults we take similar actions when we are afraid. Psychologists show that there are inbuilt responses to fear. The first is to fight, the second is to take flight, the third is to freeze. Each of these responses are inbuilt reflexes that go into action as a defence that automatically reacts to stress and trauma. We experience them in daily life, as we go into examinations, as we learn how to drive, as we give presentations, as we go for job interviews and many more situations that causes the body to respond to any form of threat. We feel the fear, the rumbling sensation in our stomachs, the inability to swallow or when our mouth goes dry and we lose the ability to speak in a coherent way. We use each of these reflexes as we come under attack or danger. Each response begins with fear and most of them originate from our childhood experiences and the memories we carry into our adult lives. When we fight back against traumatic life events there is a good chance that we will win; if not immediately, then in the future, particularly if we are persistent and do not give in to the demon of fear or the devil's attacks to reduce us to a wreckage.

Fear can be positive when it drives us to do things that we thought were impossible. Daring acts such as bungy jumping, car racing, mountain climbing and sports that carry high risk are examples that push us beyond our limits and to the edge of fear. The negative side of fear is when we go into flight or freeze mode; both positions bring negative repercussions because we feel that it is impossible to win a battle. The body's response is to release hormones to either fight or escape present danger. In that moment our reflexes tell us to be risk averse because we may not have the inward strength to contend with the danger we are exposed to. Depression and feelings of anxiety can quickly take us on a downward spiral, losing confidence and sinking into despair. Yet it is important to remember, as Proverbs 29:25 states, we are not to be fearful of Man.

The fear of Man bringeth a snare:
But who so Putteth his trust in the Lord
shall be saved

Proverbs 29:25

Freezing is when we become helpless, it is a delayed response. These responses to fear are not new and are mentioned frequently in the Bible. Two brothers, Esau and Jacob, born as twins, carried distinctly different personalities, but when Jacob stole his brother's birthright, he was forced to flee in fear. It was fear that kept Jacob from facing his brother. Thus, he carried the fear of this broken relationship for many years without reconciliation. Dale Carnegie states that it is inaction that breeds doubt and fear, but action breeds confidence and courage. Therefore, it was not until Jacob gathered the courage to face his brother that he was released from the fear that was holding him back. An outcome might not be as bad as we think, but because fear takes the leading position, we are outmanoeuvred and feel that we have lost, even when in fact we have won the battle.

When under fire to confess that he was one of Christ's followers, Peter the disciple, vehemently denied that he knew Him. It was fear that led to his denial. David, when faced with a giant, used the positive side of fear as he used a simple sling to defeat a giant. It was his courage that enabled him to put fear aside and conquer his opponent. Esther conquered fear when she had to go before the king to plead for the life of her people. She was aware that death would be her fate if the king did not hold out his sceptre to her, but she refused to be intimidated and stood up to face fear.

Imagine that you were walking through the park and suddenly you saw a snake in your path. Your first response might be to freeze in a moment of fear. If you were calm and, in that moment, devised a strategy for how to move out of the path of the snake, you would escape its assault. However, every time you visited the park, the fear would present itself, leading you to either take another route or evade returning to the park. The phobia you would develop for snakes would result in inhibition unless you could find a way to overcome the fear. Phobias do not go away easily and can result in anxiety, stress and complex behaviour patterns. Psychologists argue that fear can be debilitating because it can have a disruptive influence on a person's life.

It is good to know that there is another side of fear. It seems to me that it is about how we negotiate our way out of thinking in an irrational way. If you want to reach the point of beauty, you must exchange fear for inner peace. Anne Frank's diary speaks about how we can overcome fear. She wrote:

> The best remedy for those who are afraid, lonely or unhappy is to go outside, somewhere where they can be quite alone with the heavens, nature and God. Because only then does one feel that all is as it should be and that God wishes to see people happy, amidst the simple beauty of nature. As long as this exists, and it certainly always will, I know that then there will always be comfort for every sorrow, whatever the circumstances may be. And I firmly believe that nature brings solace in all troubles.
>
> ANNE FRANK, 1947

The Promise of Peace: The promise of peace helps us to know that whatever fears we are facing, there is peace. Jesus speaks peace to us and brings calm to threatening life experiences. This is not to say that He takes away our problems, but He gives us the grace and the fortitude to be able to cope. As the disciples battled with the storm, they were near to breaking point, but there was nowhere to flee to, so they turned to Jesus, and He metamorphosed their fear into calm. It was the type of peace that they found impossible to verbalise.

Power Displayed: There is power in fear, but it is on the other side and has positive energy. Although the disciples had seen Jesus' power displayed on numerous other occasions, they did not have the faith to believe that they could be empowered. Yet, the power they needed was just below the sinking ship. We are able to abandon any type of fear and anxiety when we are empowered to move forward in strength. As Susan Jeffers (2007) states we can feel the fear and do it anyway, by turning our fear and indecision into confidence.

I recall that several years ago, I was attending a success principles course and the trainer invited the participants to face their fears by visualising themselves being on the top of a tall building similar to a skyscraper. He invited us to feel the asphalt under our feet, walk to the edge of the building and jump off. Although it was unreal, it was nevertheless a frightening experience, but it taught me that when I am fearful, I can make a choice to be empowered, as Jesus did when he spent forty days and nights in the wilderness and was tempted by Satan. He spoke the words, 'Get thee behind me Satan.' It is only through the strength that God gives that we are able to rise from the ashes or go through the storm.

Passionate Faith: Hebrews 11:6 reminds us that without faith it is impossible to please God, therefore it is faith that is on the other side of fear and stops us from abandoning our dreams. Martin Luther King Jr. urged his followers to never give up but to fight for their freedom in his speech, 'I have a dream.' He is thus quoted:

> And as we walk, we must make the pledge that we will always march ahead. We cannot turn back.

He believed that even though his followers were fatigued as they marched, that they should abandon fear and extend their faith because he believed that 'unearned suffering is redemptive.' It is fear that urges us to give up and turn back, but equally it is faith that urges us to press forward.

Perfect Love: There are several attributes to love but one of the most poignant is that it casts out fear. In the midst of ashes or a storm the love and empathy that others demonstrate is what actually gives us a fighting spirit and the will to survive. Fear is an imposter that takes over, but love sets us free. Jesus is our best example of love, because He loved those who appeared to others to be unlovely. He loved by serving the sick, the poor and the needy. He gave a new commandment to his disciples:

> This is my commandment that ye love one another, as I have loved you.

> John 15:12

Limiting Beliefs: We may hold on to erroneous beliefs that limit us and get in the way of achieving our objectives. These beliefs are not only self-limiting, but they encourage fear to take root. We can limit the capacity that God has given us by believing the lies that others tell us. Equally, we can cling onto false beliefs through lack of self-confidence and an inability to challenge errors. We start out on life with models that justify the beliefs we hold, but over time we create a new set of beliefs that may be contradictory to the values we were taught. These beliefs come from those around us and the world views to which we are exposed. Thus, a limiting belief might challenge your right to think for yourself, it might stop you from believing that you are able to achieve your goals, or it may make you feel inferior to others. The way to challenge limiting beliefs is to recognise negative patterns that are created in your mind. You can also challenge limiting beliefs through self-reflection and self-awareness. These two processes will help to eradicate fear and stop you from believing that you are not as good as others or that you are less than others. We are told in Mark 11:23 that whatever we desire through belief will come to pass.

> ...Whosoever shall say unto this mountain, be thou removed, and be thou cast into the sea; and shall not doubt in his heart, but shall believe that those things which he saith shall come to pass; he shall have whatsoever he saith.

Food for Thought
Use the box below or your journal to reflect on the following questions.
1) How have you coped with your experience of fear from unrequited love?
2) How did fear impede your progress?
3) What did you learn and implement in your life to conquer fear?
4) What beliefs do you hold that are limiting your progress?

CHAPTER EIGHT
Strokes on the Canvas

Your life is a canvas, and every day is a brushstroke. So, make each
stroke count, and paint a masterpiece worth living.

OLUWATOBI ODUNAYO

In the vast tapestry of life, our dreams and aspirations paint vivid strokes
on our canvas of life. As an artist looks at a blank canvas, he/she must
have the desire to make deliberate strokes. However, a blank canvas can be
scary. The only way to reduce the fear is to begin by making smudges on
the canvas, that way it does not appear as if the painting is perfect. Life is
not perfect, thus as we look at the canvas, we also see that every mark
creates an impression. So, it is with everyone who wants to pursue a dream.
To gaze at the achievement of others and merely wish to emulate them is
to deny the unique potential embedded within us. The beauty comes with
an unwavering commitment to moving from trial and error to triumph.

Each person is born with the unique capability of carving out their own
path and leaving their indelible footprint on the world. Whatever the
problems we face, we must be motivated and extend faith in our capability
in times of weakness and through each storm we must have the will to
survive. The potential that is already bestowed within us must be kindled by
motivation which is the fire that gives us the spirit of endurance.

I recently visited the London Gallery and as I walked through the doors
I was amazed at the extensive collection of paintings. Some I recognised
immediately, for example, the man with the withered hand being healed by
Jesus. I saw imperfection. As I looked at the famous paintings of Rembrandt
and Van Gogh, I wondered how their canvases began and whether they
made bold or faint marks on their canvases.

Each painting told a story that began with a blank canvas but ended in
an artistic work of beauty. As my husband and I walked around the gallery,

we noticed a group of school children sitting on the floor and a teacher standing beside them giving her interpretation of what was on the canvas. She invited comments from the children about their interpretation of what was being portrayed in the painting. It was interesting to see how each child's perception of what they saw was different, yet it was one painting. It made me think about life and how some strokes are more vivid than others. In life some people face more pain and distress than others, some people go through more testing, more fires and more turbulent storms. As we began to discuss the painting in the background, my husband noticed a hand reaching out of an oval glass bowl. I protested, no, it is a man's face. He took a photograph of it and it was not until I looked at the photograph in more detail and from another angle that I saw the hand reaching out of the bowl. I realised that the painting was complex with many different themes. Life is exactly like that, because we may not always see what is on the canvas.

I have never felt the urge to draw or paint, but a few years ago I attended a women's event at which I was the keynote speaker. During the afternoon the group were given a task to work in pairs and draw the impressions on the wall on our blank canvases. I was at a loss and did not know where to begin, but as we engaged in conversation, I noticed that my partner's painting took on a beautiful shape. I felt ashamed because I was unable to create a painting, soon my canvas was a blur of colours. Over the next two years I did not stop thinking of the blank canvas and one day I decided to take online classes with an artist. One of the things he constantly repeated to the group of learners was that life is like a canvas but in beginning to make the first stroke you must make some smudges. It made me think that although we are born with a blank canvas it soon gets messy, but it is the only way to learn. It was after experiencing failure, I experienced success when I drew my first sketch of a lioness and her cub.

Despite facing challenges, we must remain motivated and believe in our capability to survive each messy patch. It is the potential within us that is ignited by motivation and a belief in a God of possibilities. In life's tapestry, our dreams and aspirations paint vivid strokes on our canvas.

In the following narrative a picture is painted of a woman's canvas that holds pain, suffering, abuse and loneliness.

Amina's Canvas of Domestic Abuse

Through all my failed relationships education was the beauty that I got out of it. I always think, and I always say, that there is always another way if this is not for me there is another path for me to get there.

Amina was raised in a strict Muslim family. As a child, she dreamed of becoming a lawyer. However, her aspirations took a different turn at the end of senior school when her parents opposed further education. Instead, she was forced to embrace the path of marriage at a young age. In compliance with her parent's wishes, she saw her future as having many children and as having a big table with a happy family sitting around it in unity. Her aspirations to move on to further education and be self-supporting were not realised as she had hoped. Yet, Amina maintained an industrious spirit, purchasing a flat and starting a small business that flourished for a while.

The Ashes Experience: Amina's life took a turn for the worse after she discovered that her husband was an asylum seeker without leave to remain in the UK. At the time she did not know what being an asylum seeker meant. Unaware of the challenges that lay ahead, her husband's descent into alcohol misuse, unfaithfulness, domestic abuse, verbal aggression and financial mismanagement shattered her dreams. She had two children from this relationship, but she struggled to care for them single-handedly. The magnitude of her problems led her to sink into depression.

Her husband's destructive habits led him to gamble away their finances, spending the money she had earned on other women, some of them visiting her home while she slept alone. In desperation she took out a second mortgage, only to lose her home and the small business which she had created as a result of her own initiative. Amina stated that his unfaithfulness was the most hurtful part of her journey. Amina felt utterly alone after her marriage came to an end. Her description of this episode was thus:

I was in a dark place. I couldn't talk to my parents, I was bankrupt, I had lost everything. I suffered verbal abuse and financial abuse and I ended up completely bankrupt. I lost my home; I lost my business, and I was completely alone. I had never been exposed to anything of this nature before marriage. I thought that my husband would take care of me, but he was an alcoholic, and he would spend all his money on gambling. I didn't realise until bills started coming through the door. His reaction to my challenges resulted in threats, lots of swearing and lots of verbal abuse.

Isolated and without any other form of help, Amina was advised by her parents to marry for a second time, because it was considered to be a family disgrace for a Muslim woman to be living on her own as a single parent. Against her best judgement, Amina was married for a second time, but this relationship crumbled. For a second time Amina experienced a failed relationship after she discovered that her husband was living a double life. On discovering his true identity Amina confronted him, and he admitted his dishonesty and walked out the door. Without support, she stood on the streets with nothing but bags in her hands and with her two children by her side. In desperation and looking for shelter, she was forced to disclose to her father that her marriage had ended. Broken and destitute, she was forced to return to the family home.

Eventually she was introduced to an older man who became her third husband, but she stated that they were married for different reasons. She confessed:

I wanted my parents off my back and he wanted to show his parents that he was with someone.

However, Amina decided that she did not want to have any more children because she wanted to become independent. Her husband was a coach driver, and he had a massive road traffic accident that left him paralysed placing her in the role of a care-giver. He was advised by doctors that he would not have children, but against the odds, Amina became pregnant with her third child.

Amina's experience of domestic abuse was multifaceted: she faced infidelity, emotional abuse, exploitation and social isolation. Unravelling her feelings, Amina spoke about the numbness and robotic existence she was leading as she silently endured unimaginable turmoil. She said:

When I look back, it was awful, I was so numb, I often think that I was in a robotic mode, it was only when it had finished that I told Dad, because I had nowhere to go.

Amina questioned herself about the purpose of her life. It was through this soul searching that she decided to study because education was always at the forefront of her mind. She said, 'I went back to education when I was in my thirties.' Amina broke free of her ashes when she gained her first degree in psychology and criminology and went on to complete a master's degree. This was the time when her ashes turned to beauty.

Amina's Journey: The Quest of Beauty in Education

Determined to break free of her parents' lack of encouragement, Amina pursued her dreams and fought to raise her children and rebuild her life through the pursuit of education. Yet her parents refused to support her and insisted that she was incapable of achieving. Nevertheless, against a seemingly hopeless situation she succeeded. She supported and encouraged her son to study, and he gained a degree of which she could feel proud. Amina's educational journey ignited her passion for social work, leading her to first take up a position working with children. Through her experience she became a passionate supporter of women suffering domestic abuse.

Amina's resilience was rooted in the power of prayer and in the power of education. Of prayer she stated:

Praying is a way of sharing, because you can be honest, because not everyone is willing to listen, but when I pray, I feel as if I am being listened to, so I hold that very close to my heart.

Of education she said:

Every hurdle is an opportunity to learn and grow.

The way to overcome was to find peace and this way of responding to her difficulties allowed Amina to reach a stage of acceptance so that she could take the next step. She was able to say:

Throughout every hurdle I have had to pick myself up, accept what had happened and be at peace; it is only then that I could take the next step. If I had never been exposed to alcohol and domestic abuse, I would not be able to understand what families are going through. In any aspect of life unless you are able to understand your emotions you will not be able to move on.

Amina had a complex family history and in later life her parents separated. She became a source of support for them without retaliating or judging them for the way they had treated her.

Reflecting on Amina's Journey

Education was the way Amina broke free of the cycle of abuse. Reflecting on her journey, she emphasised the key role that education played in her transformation as she rose from ashes to beauty. It was her relentless pursuit of knowledge that became a pathway to independence and a source of strength in overcoming adversity.

As I reflect on Amina's story these are the nuggets I gathered from her narrative. Each nugget is worthy of sharing with every person who has the desire to overcome and achieve their aspirations.

The first nugget we can draw from her experience was her exposure to the dysfunctional and turbulent relationship she endured with her parents, whose expectations were low and mediocre. It was their disbelief that she could achieve and reach her true potential that threw her off course. Even as an adult they were unable to celebrate her successes refusing to attend her graduation. Nevertheless, she was able to turn her hurdles into sources of strength. Her ability to understand and empathise with others enabled her to navigate difficult situations that negatively impacted her health and wellbeing. Her response and inner resources eventually led to the support and comfort she was able to give to others.

The second nugget was her ability to achieve peace in the midst of the storm. This brought calm into her life and helped her to survive considerable turmoil and unhappiness, even though for a time she had lost sight of her aspirations and could not see the lighthouse in the distance.

The third nugget is that she accepted what had happened and while not being passive, she empowered herself, moving on to change what was painted on her canvas. Her journey involved learning from each hurdle, making conscious choices to move forward rather than dwell on the past. It was her relentless pursuit of education and her determination that eventually led to her success.

The fourth nugget is that while she faced negativity and a lack of love and support from her parents, she chose not to internalise their judgments and low expectations. Instead, she emerged stronger, creating her definition of success and beauty. She perceives her achievements, including her job, her son's degree, as beauty that came out of ashes. Even the lessons learned from failed relationships contributed to this beauty. Each hurdle she faced became an opportunity for growth, learning and transformation.

The fifth nugget was her experience of domestic abuse. This was an area of her life where she lacked personal autonomy. She was reduced to feeling like a robot. The impact of abuse took her on a roller-coaster journey where she was unable to speak of its debilitating effect. Nevertheless, her quest was to use education as a conduit to excellence.

The sixth nugget is that she demonstrates that life is a continuous learning journey. I found that education served as a force, propelling her forward to make a profound difference, not only in her life but in the lives of others through her commitment and wish to be of service. Her philosophy of life was centred on continuous learning, whether it was connected to broken and destructive relationships, facing failure, homelessness, and lack of support, isolation, negative judgments or learning from her parents' negative valuations. In each situation, she was able to draw on the lessons she had learnt from her teacher when she was thirteen years old. It was the story of footprints in the sand, and it became a lasting symbol of connection, reminding her that she was not alone on her journey.

> One night a man had a dream. He dreamed he was walking along the beach with the Lord. Across the sky, flashed scenes from his life. For each scene he noticed two sets of footprints in the sand; one belonged to him and the other to the Lord.
>
> When the last scene of his life flashed before him, he looked back at the footprints in the sand. He noticed that many times along the path of his life there was only one set of footprints. He also noticed that it also happened at the very lowest and saddest times of his life.
>
> This really bothered him, and he questioned the Lord about it. 'Lord, you said that once I decided to follow you, you'd walk with me all the way. But I have noticed that during the most troublesome times in my life, there is only one set of footprints. I don't understand why, when I needed you most, you would leave me.'
>
> The Lord replied, 'My precious, precious child, I love you and I would never leave you. During your times of trial and suffering, when you see only one set of footprints, it was then that I carried you.'
>
> MARY STEVENSON

Integral to Amina's survival was the role that prayer played in her life. She was able to say that praying helped her to feel listened to and comforted, thus she held prayer close to her heart. Matthew 21:22 states:

> And all things, whatsoever ye ask in prayer, believing ye shall receive.

Amina's metamorphosis from a caterpillar to a butterfly symbolises her strength and resilience. Her story shows that even when our lives are reduced to ashes it is possible to emerge with strength, wisdom and a sense of beauty. In the end, no one can take that form of beauty from us because it comes from within.

Highlights based on Amina's Story

- Never give up
- Remember that there is always a way
- When you feel as if no one will listen pray and ask God for discernment
- Think of the positives and move on
- Learn the art of acceptance and do not see it as a weakness but a strength
- Every day brings new learning, so learn as much as you can, do not sit around and dwell on mistakes you have made
- Look for what connects you with others and what brings peace into your life
- Remember that peace brings beauty.

Food For Thought

In the space below or using your journal consider

1) What you have learnt from Amina's story.
2) How did her response change her narrative from ashes to beauty?
3) Make a note of your talents/gifts and how these can help you to build your character.

CHAPTER NINE

The Crucible of Despair

But he knoweth the way that I take: When he hath tried me, I shall come forth as gold.

Job 23:10

There are times when we not only face the storm but also the fire. Both have the capacity to destroy but both point to the possibility of a new and transformed life. The crucible of despair is a type of burning and a melting process with fervent heat. Metaphorically speaking the crucible brings severe testing but it also leads to refinement. It is like gold that is severely tested in the fire, but it emerges as a metal with great value. In Job's experience he considered his life to be tested by fire.

Undoubtedly, burning results in loss and dross. The life experiences of Job led him to contend that even when his friends were against him, he knew that God would bring him out of the fire victoriously.

The apostle Paul reminds us that even though a man's work is burned through testing he will suffer loss of his reward, nevertheless he will be saved by the fire (1 Corinthians 3:15). The crucible can come through water or fire, but Isaiah 43:2 states that God will save us in both situations.

When you pass through the waters, I will be with you; And through the rivers they shall not overflow you. When you walk through the fire, you shall not be burned, nor shall the flame scorch you.

Isaiah 43:2

When a person is going through the crucible of despair there is complete loss and absence of hope. It is an experience that is often accompanied by fear, discouragement and hopelessness which is contained within the crucible or container where the fire is intense or within the leaking boat where the waters threaten to destroy.

It is the challenges of both elements over which we do not have control that induces deep feelings of helplessness. Martin Seligman (1975), an American psychologist known for his extensive contribution to positive psychology, promoted self-help as a strategy for overcoming helplessness. After he conducted experiments with dogs, he unexpectedly found that after they were conditioned to certain stimuli, they did not respond when opportunities arose for them to escape. He named this phenomenon "learned helplessness". There are other examples of this response in human beings.

Donald Clifton spent many years researching the strange phenomenon that caused prisoners of war in a Japanese concentration camp to die or discontinue contact with fellow officers and family after they had been released. He discovered that the Japanese did not confine, brutalise nor starve the soldiers, instead, they committed an atrocity called psychological warfare. The soldiers were asked to confess their wrongdoing to each other, to be self-critical, to be disloyal and to withhold all emotional support from their compatriots. As they became vulnerable, disrespectful and suspicious of each other they also lost trust and the bond they had developed with each other irretrievably broke down. A crucible was created to induce fear, so that even after the soldiers had been released, and were given the opportunity to call their relatives, none of them took the opportunity to do so, and neither did they maintain any friendships or relationships with each other.

Clifton concluded that they had learned how to be helpless. A similar situation exists in cases of domestic abuse, where the abuser's control over the abused leads them to develop an unhealthy relationship with the abuser. A relationship is developed that destroys self-esteem and can lead to depression and other mental health conditions. It was a lack of resistance and motivation to fight back that brought about the soldier's untimely demise. Where there is silence, the perpetrator is able to increase their power base through subjugation, domination and manipulation.

In their book, *How Full is Your Bucket?* Tom Rath and Donald Clifton (2004), enlighten our understanding of what they termed "bucket dipping". We can use the dipper from our bucket to fill up another person's bucket by giving them love, care, and understanding and by being empathic. However, the dipper can be used to deplete another person's resources. We can only give if our buckets are full but when there is a leak, similar to a leaking boat, we can resort to dipping from another person's bucket. By dipping from another person's bucket, the intention is to drain their inner resources, thus making them feel ineffectual, by reducing their confidence and self-efficacy.

I found that the crucible of fire was present in Clarissa's story as she described a journey that led to ashes. In her description of the ashes experience was a clear link between helplessness, empowerment and resilience.

Clarissa's Journey: From Burnout to Breakthrough

When I think of what ashes means I think of having gone through a fire and as a result, aspects of your life are burnt up and destroyed and you have lost everything, and it looks as if all hope is lost.

Clarissa was in her early twenties when a pivotal chapter in her life unfolded. She had successfully completed her first degree and had a bright future. However, what followed was an unforeseen plunge into burnout, total exhaustion and mental turmoil. Clarissa could not have foreseen the steep decline into mental health problems; neither was she prepared for a sudden collapse when, in the presence of her friends, she had a mental breakdown. The condition she suddenly experienced left her delirious. Misunderstood by those around her she found herself facing hospital admission. It was then that the unwavering intuition of her mother's prayers became an example of spiritual insight that penetrated through the darkness. Clarissa was bedridden and incapacitated for several months but her first response was to begin to pray. It was during this time that her mother offered a lifeline to understanding her condition amidst her chaos and confusion. Her worst fear was that she would be unable to continue her studies or regain the capacity to stand.

Clarissa's aspirations of pursuing a master's degree faded and crumbled under the weight of mental instability. She commented:

I had seemingly lost everything, that is what I think about ashes, I couldn't walk and my brain just shut down, and all hope was gone.

Bedridden and despondent, she became sceptical about ever regaining a normal life. Interwoven with Clarissa's ashes experience was fear and relentless adversity that held her in a vice-like grip to the point where it became impossible to have any rest or to sleep. Sensing her distress during the dark hours, Clarissa's mother began to sleep in her bedroom to quell the nightmares through the harrowing hours of sleeplessness. A verse of scripture suddenly came to mind, and it was that God gives his beloved sleep.

> It is vain for you to rise up early, to sit up late, to eat the bread of sorrows: for so he giveth his beloved sleep.
>
> Psalms 127:2

It was this verse that allowed her to claim the promise of sleep and to resist over-dependence on her mother's help. It proved to be the beginning of a long journey back to health.

From Ashes to Beauty

> I will bless the LORD at all times: his praise shall continually be in my mouth.
> My soul shall make her boast in the LORD: the humble shall hear thereof, and be glad. O magnify the LORD with me, and let us exalt his name together. I sought the LORD, and he heard me, and delivered me from all my fears.
>
> Psalm 34:1-4

Clarissa emerged from her sudden and unexplained illness when she summoned strength from an unexplored reservoir. Guided by the words and unconditional love of her mother, she gained strength that was needed to stand on her feet again. Anchored in faith she stood up to the mental condition that was reducing her to a state of fear, and the inability to rest. It was a pivotal moment of reclaiming her autonomy and defying the dark shadows that had tormented her thoughts.

Clarissa's journey was not only about spiritual ascent, but it was a testament to the symbiosis of her combined faith and action. She stated that there came a time when the door of her faith led to the realisation of her need to stand on the bedrock of God's promises. She recognised the necessity of becoming proactive and became determined in her fight to regain control over the thoughts that told her that she was an old woman when she gazed at herself in the mirror. Each deliberate step she took moved her forward with an unmovable belief that in the darkest moment of her crucible she would emerge from the ashes. It was the strength to take action, it was at her weakest point, that healing came. It also brought an enriched understanding of her fragility and at the same time, the power that lies within.

Clarissa's stated definition of ashes transcended the conventional as she discovered that there was a profound grace that enabled her to regain her mental capacity. Her definition was linked to discernment and the right to reclaim control over her thought processes. In so doing she rose from the depths of despair and mental turmoil. She found solace in hope. On her journey to recovery, Clarissa reignited her love for knowledge and the aspirations she had to continue her studies resulted in distinctions and accolades for her research.

At the pinnacle of her journey came success in her studies, leading to professional and business acumen. She transitioned from the role of auditor, climbing the ranks and crafting a billion-pound government strategy from a blank sheet. She states that it was God's guidance that propelled her to develop innovative solutions and achieve organisational objectives for the project she was leading. Yet the most profound beauty that emerged was her forgiveness of those who had condemned and judged her as mentally deficient. To those who pronounced judgment came a transcendent act of forgiveness and as a result, she was release from negative feelings.

In the crucible of Clarissa's experience came the restoration of her health. She stated:

> *God not only restored my mental faculties but also granted me opportunities that seemed inconceivable.*

Reflecting on Clarissa's Journey

Clarissa presented as a confident woman who went through a severe mental test. In the absence of support from those around her, she found her mother to be a stalwart of support and a loyal friend. Her story demonstrates the gift of discernment as she made the choice to defy the negative messages she was told and her determination to stand up and walk. It was her thirst for knowledge that was of key importance throughout her journey. Her story shows that when a person is going through extreme stress it can lead to burnout which inevitably impacts mental functioning. She had not only lost her mental faculties, but also the capacity to walk. In a split second she moved from a position of high expectations to a place where she had lost her health, and the dreams she had cultivated in her mind.

The most profound beauty in her story was the capacity to forgive, which brought a sense of closure and peace. It is often said that we cannot forget the wrongs that others have done to us, but we can make a choice to move on and learn from our human experiences. Desmond and Mpho Tutu (2014) wrote that the path to forgiveness is not an easy one, but in order to do it, we must 'shake off hatred and anger and make our way through grief and loss to find acceptance that is the very essence of forgiveness.'

The key to Clarissa's transformative journey lay in anchoring herself on God's promises. She found hope that was fuelled by her faith and through Divine guidance. It was this combination that paved the way and gave her courage to face her fears.

As I reflect on Clarissa's journey, it is apparent that she made a leap from mental illness, to auditor, to strategist, from brokenness to achievement and from fear to courage. Her transformation came through the power of unwavering faith, hope, familial support and limitless grace of God's power. Her quest for beauty was actualised when she changed her thinking processes.

Overcoming fear is a task demanding courage. It requires us to confront, refute and stare down the demon of doubt. As we take tentative steps, they become determined strides and with each stride comes the realisation that we are stronger than we ever imagined. A journey that holds fear loses its grip, loss and sadness moves us towards the light. The turning point arrives when we discover the latent power that lies within ourselves to make our way back from darkness to light, from ashes to beauty. It is the spirit of optimism that becomes a catalytic converter for change.

Highlights Based on Clarissa's Story

- When you are feeling fearful think of the opposite of fear which is hope
- Anchor yourself in positive thoughts
- Forgive unconditionally
- Remember that God has the power to orchestrate all the events in your life
- Make life-style changes to support optimum health
- Learn about the impact of stress and how to reduce it
- Seek help if you are depressed, look for services in your community
- Find people who can support you and help you to recover
- Always hope in possibilities not impossibilities
- Immerse yourself in the word of God where you will find promises for good health
- Remember that the crucible of despair will eventually come to an end.

Food for Thought

Task: Use your reflective journal or the box below to contemplate the following questions

1) Write a letter to God and put your requests, whatever they might be, to Him.
2) Write about a fearful experience in your life, and how you coped with it
3) What lessons did you learn from it?

CHAPTER TEN

Walking Through the Fire and the Storm

If I take the wings of the morning, and dwell in the uttermost parts of the sea; Even there shall thy hand lead me, And thy right hand shall hold me. If I say, Surely the darkness shall cover me; Even the night shall be light about me. Yea, the darkness hideth not from thee; but the night shineth as the day: the darkness and the light are both alike to thee.

Psalms 139:9-12

There are times in our lives when we must walk through the storm and the fire. Both present us with challenges that we may think are insurmountable. These types of experiences feel as if they will never come to an end. It may appear as if no beauty is possible even if we are searching diligently for it. It is important to remember that the burning that results from the fire will come to an end, the rain that comes with the storm will eventually stop and the rainbow will appear. The problems we experience come in many different ways, some of them too numerous to mention, but we know them because we feel them. When we are walking through the storm and the fire, God gives us an invitation to place our hand in His hand. The best realisation is to remember that God is the master of the fire and the storm, He is in them and He has control over them.

There is no place we can run and hide from God, as the Psalmist David discovered. We cannot go anywhere that is impossible for Him to penetrate and find us. The above verse gives me the assurance that God is ever present in our sorrows, and in our joys. He sees everything and He knows all things because He is the Alpha and Omega, the beginning and the end.

Some years ago, my son and I were visiting my sister, who was at the time living in Boston USA. We decided to take a trip to Martha's Vineyard in Massachusetts. The trip involved taking a boat across to the island. It was fair weather when we set out on the trip. Our hope was to have a memorable day exploring the delights of this beautiful island cut off from the mainland. We could not have expected that the weather would change drastically. However, on our way back the captain announced that a storm was on its way. We arrived at the shore but had quite some miles to drive before we could arrive home.

During that time, the storm was gathering momentum, the winds were playing havoc with the car, its force was stronger and mightier than us and the car. We knew that the danger was present, but our only solution was to let go of the fear and allow the master of the storm to take control. Our best weapon was to pray. The journey home was tortuous, we feared for our lives, but my sister's skill for driving helped us to reach our destination safely. We believed that it was our commitment to give over the situation to the Lord that calmed our nerves and took away the anxiety.

> Do not be anxious about anything, but in everything by prayer and supplication with thanksgiving let your request be made known to God.
>
> Philippians 4:6

Having arrived home safely we gave thanks. The lesson for me was the need to always give thanks, remembering to show gratitude for the blessing that God daily gives us. Prayer is a strong contender at any time but particularly when we are at our weakest point. Prayer encourages us to let go and wait on God for an answer.

Hannah was a childless woman; her story is recorded in the book of 1 Samuel 1 and 2. She had a desire to have a child. In her struggles she prayed for a son and waited patiently on God to give her an answer. Her prayers were answered with the birth of Samuel, who became one of the greatest prophets in Bible history. We can learn from her story in so far as she was prepared to pray and wait on God. She was not disappointed because He blessed her abundantly. This story teaches us about how to be obedient under extreme conditions.

On 14th January 2017 a tower block called Grenfell in West London caught fire and seventy-one people were burnt in the flames. I watched the news as this sad and horrifying story unfolded. In the days to come we were told that the fire raged for sixty hours, taking the lives of seventy people and leaving the ashes of their remains buried at the site. It was described as the deadliest fire in the United Kingdom since the German bombing during World War II. Yet, 223 people escaped the ashes and their lives were saved.

As well as facing the flames we may face the flood. Such was the case of the 2004 tsunami in Thailand that came without warning and took the lives of thousands of people, causing fear and distress in its wake. The impact of fires, storms, tsunamis and earthquakes across the globe comes with destructive force. The question to ask is how do we bounce back from this level of disaster? The first action that the people of Thailand took was to begin rebuilding their damaged homes and communities. Government support was provided to enable small communities to begin reconstructing their lives. Since the tourist industry was hit by the disaster, they began to fight back to reconstruct the industry that was their livelihood. The families in the Grenfell tower disaster did a similar thing as they made their voices heard, as did the New Orleans community that has been severely hit by violent storms. It is a human need to return to the site of our pain and remember those we have lost, all too often before their appointed time.

The following narrative demonstrates how it is possible to cultivate hope after disaster strikes with unrelenting force.

Janine's Story: Battling Depression

Having calamities is about acceptance. You can question it and say why is this happening to me. But with hope you have confidence that everything is happening for a moment. If you try your best to be strong, resilient and patient hoping that you are going to get through it, you will come out of it stronger to face other challenges.

Janine's story is an illustration of how walking through a metaphorical fire or storm can be destructive but can also bring positive results. It largely depends on how we think and the actions we take to reach the point of recovery.

Janine was at university in her third year and was overwhelmed by the pressure of studying. The more she pushed herself, the less she became able to spot the warning signs of mental illness, because she desperately wanted to achieve her goal of gaining a degree. Meanwhile, her immune system was under attack and was failing to keep pace with the stress she was undergoing. Her illness first began when she noticed bouts of depression. At the same time that she was going through this ordeal, she met a man who became her husband. While they were dating, she discovered that he was living in the UK illegally and she fell apart at the prospect of losing him. It was the first time that Janine had an experience of depression and it led her to feel as if she was at sea and drowning. She simply did not know what recovery would look or feel like.

At the age of twenty, Janine experienced a profound encounter with severe anxiety leading to clinical depression. Primarily she lacked awareness of its underlying cause but sensed that it would change her life. She found herself at a complete low point, unable to sleep and feeling as if her brain was 'physically hurting'. This condition persisted for many months, evolving into a debilitating cycle of fear. Initially, she turned to medication to alleviate her symptoms, but as its effectiveness waned, she resorted to an overdose in a desperate attempt to find relief to compensate for her lack of sleep. Panic attacks plagued her nights, rendering any enjoyment during the day impossible. Her overall quality of life plummeted, and she even contemplated stopping eating as a means of escaping her suffering, but her mother dissuaded her from taking this action.

Experiencing intense and overwhelming darkness, Janine vividly recalls standing on a railway bridge, contemplating suicide, feeling that she no longer wanted to exist. Janine was in the depths of suicidal thoughts, grappling with the difficulty of her situation and struggling to envision a way out of the seemingly insurmountable challenges, unable to see any light at the end of her tunnel.

Ever since her first experience Janine has had bouts of severe clinical depression, but she states that the longer they persisted, the harder it was to find a way out of them. It is now five years since Janine has been suffering and although she has episodes of normality there are also times when she has breakdowns. She discovered that stopping the medication was unhelpful.

Janine is the mother of three children. She feels that her illness had an impact on her last child because she had a bout of severe depression when she was pregnant with him and did not think that she would survive this experience because of the negative thoughts that invaded her mind. She continued to tell herself that she was a bad person and did not know if she would love her child when he was born. Despite the odds, Janine continued to take the prescribed medication and it eventually worked to her benefit.

Janine came to the point of acceptance and surrender during the Covid-19 pandemic when her mother became ill with bipolar disorder and was hospitalised. As a result, she lost the support she heavily relied on. She felt lost and was drowning in deep waters and to add to matters she felt completely on her own. It was a battle that caused her to fight for survival.

As Janine became isolated and alone, she began to think of ways to rise above her adversity; she resurrected her love of nature and jogging. Janine found a way to accept that there would be bad days but told herself that it would not stay that way. She began to believe her experience was shaping her as a person and giving her the skills to cope – and not just cope but excel and know that she could be happy even as a person with a mental health condition.

Janine stated that it was realisation and acceptance, while not anticipating the negative, but seeing that it was a process of refinement. Janine believes that the ashes experience she went through made her stronger. Nevertheless, she confessed that her experience felt like ashes because it seemed impossible to recover. She said:

It was so difficult, I had nothing left and I thought, how am I going to get myself out of this situation and I thought it was impossible, impossible.

Janine's faith has always been a strong part of who she is, and she found that it was her faith that stopped her from declining into the destructive thoughts leading her to believe that committing suicide was the answer. She continued:

I got to the point where one sleeping tablet wasn't working and one night, I think I ended up taking more because I wanted to sleep. I was panicking at night-time and I couldn't enjoy anything during the day … I remember telling my parents that my quality of life had just gone, it just finished.

She was able to say that even though she went through hard times, it was for a reason, and it allowed her to have a deeper understanding of her identity. Thinking of how she came to the point of beauty she stated that it was reaching a stage of acceptance and positive thinking:

It was acceptance. I am positive. I accepted that I was going to have bad days but not stay like that and knowing that my experience was shaping me and giving me the skills to cope and not just cope but excel. It was knowing that you can be happy even when you have a mental health problem.

Furthermore, she stated that with her distress came beauty, because she was able to love her son. The challenge after his birth was having to care for a child with a learning disability. She was able to see the beauty because of her belief system:

I am a firm believer in the fact that nobody likes these tests, but there is goodness in them because of who you become as a person.

Paul the Apostle states:

Now faith is the substance of things hoped for, the evidence of things not seen.

Hebrews 11:1

Eventually the beauty came and was akin to seeing the impossible materialise. It was at this point that Janine began to see good coming out of a bad situation. There was a new level of faith and with it there came the will to fight back against the challenges she was facing. Thinking back to her experience Janine confessed that her world changed as she took actions based on self-healing principles, such as dieting, exercising, and enjoying nature. She redefined her experience from a negative to a positive one. Janine's husband received leave to stay, her marriage survived and today her husband is an integral part of her support network.

Reflection on Janine's Story

As I spoke with Janine, it was clear that she is a bright and vivacious woman, but she had undergone an unbearable experience. The decline of a person's mental health is one of the illnesses that we do not fully understand. We do not have a full appreciation of how the mind works and why some people are affected more than others by anxiety which can lead to clinical depression. Alongside her depression was a pregnancy that produced negative thoughts as to whether she could love her child. Her quest for beauty became real when she chose to love her son who was born with a disability. At the same time, she had two children who needed her care and attention. Stress was one of the factors that led to mental ill health as well as her mother's history of bipolar disease.

At the onset of her illness, Janine was coping with two stressful life events. She was under pressure to complete her studies. She was focusing on gaining a qualification to improve her life chances and did not spot the signs and symptoms of her illness. At the same time, she had an opportunity to be happy but the man she had chosen as a partner brought the complex problem into her life of being an illegal immigrant. She was placed in the position where she feared losing him, but it was a trigger that resulted from stress. She was under pressure and did not know how to resolve it at the time. The problems she faced manifested themselves during the pandemic. It was a time when support systems had disappeared. Concomitantly with her personal distress, she lost the support of her mother to a mental health problem, which heightened her fear. It appeared to push her into a position where she was forced to fight back against the forces of her illness.

Janine did not allow the test she faced to push her overboard. Even though she came to the brink and the end of her resources, she instead became resilient because she wanted to get the most out of life. In order to achieve this goal, she needed to possess the strength to live rather than die. In this regard, she set out on a course to make the most out of life. She chose to possess hope because she stated that, *'hope brings positivity, knowing that you will come out stronger to face other challenges.'*

There were steps that Janine took that we can learn from. The first was how she began to physically exercise even though at times she felt suicidal.

Magna Parks-Porterfield (2007), a psychologist, states that exercise 'does wonders for our mental health' because it releases chemicals that improve how we feel. These chemicals enhance our moods, they reduce anxiety and give us a greater sense of wellbeing. Further, she states that there are other benefits to exercise, among which is an increase of stamina to overcome stress. As Janine went jogging it helped her to develop a more positive outlook because, in time, it improved her chances of a healthy body and brain. Another strategy that became significant for Janine was prayer. She states:

> *Prayer was also incredibly important because when I put my head down on the floor, I remember just crying, crying and crying and asking for help; even though I was going through that darkest horrible time I still felt that I was going to get help.*

Self-Care

Babies are born with an incredible ability to self-care by soothing themselves. They begin by rootling and sucking. As adults we lose sight of the natural ability to care for ourselves. We overwork and push our bodies to the limit. We forget the importance of rest, exercise, fresh air, water, meditation, prayer and generally we do not take care of our body, which is our greatest gift and greatest asset.

The ability to take the time to reflect is often missing from our lives. There are many people that do not know how to take time to reflect and meditate on a daily basis. Reflection brings many benefits because it encourages us to look at ourselves and make adjustments where it is necessary. It helps in looking at our coping strategies and how we manage difficult situations as well as to become aware of the types of behaviours that impact our general wellbeing.

Self-reflection brings peace and a sense of calm. I started journaling as a way of reflecting and over the years I have found it to be a positive way of letting go of the things that make me feel anxious and worried. As I begin to write, it allows me to express my feelings through the written Word. I find this an effective way to take care of my health. As a lecturer I taught reflective practice and found that students did not understand what it meant to engage in reflection because it calls for introspection by exploring our emotions and behaviour; nevertheless, it is an effective way to self-care.

Meditation provides us with the space to let go of the daily hassles and concentrate from the inside out. For Christians and believers, meditation means taking time to dwell on and learn from God's Word. It allows us to spend quiet time reflecting on God's goodness and giving gratitude for each day with the realisation that every breath we take comes from the hand of a merciful and loving Father.

Highlights based on Janine's advice

- Don't shut yourself in, get out and exercise
- Carry on doing the things you used to do
- Don't say I can't do it, but I will do it
- Strive for the best you can possibly be
- Do something positive for yourself like looking at and enjoying nature
- Talk to positive people not negative people because negative people can pull you down
- In order to get out of the blip the first thing to do is take care of the basic things such as hygiene, and physical needs
- Be motivated to make yourself fresh
- Eat well, don't have caffeine because it can make you feel worse

- Have regular bedtimes and a daily routine
- If you are having problems sleeping have a hot bath, treat yourself – self-care.

Food for Thought

This activity will help you to think about your emotions and the role they play in your health. Use the box below to

1) Record some of the emotions you feel when you experience times of anxiety
2) Based on Janine's advice which activities can you engage in to help you feel better?
3) If you know someone suffering with depression, how would you recognise the signs and symptoms and what actions would you take to help them battle the storm by coping with anxiety?

CHAPTER ELEVEN

The Master of the Ship: Responding to Setbacks

From a spiritual point of view, the true master of your ship is Christ himself. It is He who brings abundance into your life. From a human point of view, however, you are the master of your ship since you need to make choices and decisions that will be of benefit to you. You may start out on the sea of life with good intentions, but life is not as straightforward as we would like it to be. Thus, there is a stark difference between these two masters, because Christ deals in impossibilities and knows the beginning from the end. He is able to help you confront and deal with what can seem impossible for you to do. He is the captain, He is the anchor, He is the lighthouse, in short, He is everything that keeps you afloat. When you accept Christ as the master of your ship you will recognise His complete all-sufficiency and ability to control everything that happens to you.

Consider the story in Luke 5:4-6 where we are told that Simon Peter had been fishing all night and did not catch any fish; but Jesus said to him, 'Launch out into the deep and let down your nets'. It was after Peter cast out his nets in obedience that there was a significant and unexpected catch. Although Peter was able to take his boat out to sea looking for fish, as the captain he toiled without having success until Jesus intervened and dealt with the setback he was experiencing. Jesus gave Peter permission to walk on the water. He was given the authority to make the leap, but he took his eyes off Jesus and began to sink. In that moment Jesus stretched out his hand and saved him. Jesus's response to Peter was thus spoken: 'Oh, thou of little faith wherefore didst thou doubt.' Matthew 13:31.

When Jonah was given a mission by God to go to Nineveh he went to the bottom of the ship and slept. The captain realised that he was not in control of the ship and that the entire crew would sink. Jonah suggested that he should be thrown overboard, and it was after this action that God restored control to the captain, saving all on board. Jonah took a downward path because of his resistance and lack of obedience. He was unwilling to unite with God's plan, and it led him into the belly of the fish. Not only did Jonah lack spiritual faith, but his mindset was far from what God wanted him to accomplish, namely love those who were different to himself. (See Jonah chapters 1–4.)

In the next story Olivia had to deal with a significant and unexpected setback that changed her life completely.

Olivia's Story

When I think of ashes, I think of something that has burnt completely, when you put your hands through it, it is like flour and there is nothing left of the original substance.

Olivia was born in the United Kingdom and her mother became ill shortly after she was born. This illness was brought on by her father's infidelity, which led to their separation. Her mother's descent into mental illness meant that Olivia was now living with her father, and he was unable to cope with parenting. At the age of two, she was placed in a residential home, until she was eight years old. Eventually, her father removed her from residential care and took her to her mother's country of birth.

Olivia recounted this experience as a challenging time in her life, but even more challenging was when she became pregnant at the age of thirteen and became a teen parent. Reflecting on her ashes, she defined it as a powdery substance when nothing is left. She perceived beauty as being in the 'eyes of the beholder', but her ashes experience was when she 'could not see the end of the tunnel.'

The once loving relationship she relished with her father disintegrated after he discovered that she was pregnant. She states that her father decided that she could no longer stay in his home, due ostensibly to the shame he felt. As a result, she was thrown out on the streets to find her way in life.

Homeless, destitute and feeling abandoned, she found herself in a desperate situation, walking the streets, and sitting in a park all day long. She was unable to return to school and lost out on an education.

During her months of pregnancy Olivia longed to end her life. She felt ashamed and lacked support from those who were closest to her. Suicidal thoughts haunted her and drove her to engage in self-harming and risky behaviours. She said:

> *I was suicidal because I had no support at all, not from the father of my child or my father, I had to hide. I was telling God that now is the time to take me.*

Day after day, Olivia focused on how she could create a situation to bring about a miscarriage. In desperation she jumped off a bench and engaged in other self-harming behaviours. Feelings of her body being invaded by her baby haunted her thoughts to the point where she wanted to lose her child. Yet none of the actions she took were successful.

It was during this time of utter loneliness that she was approached by a woman, a stranger who noticed that she was alone, and befriended her by offering her a place to stay. As if the memory was hard to bear, she said:

> *I think that was the worst time in my life. I couldn't manage the situation; it was a terrible situation. I found myself homeless, walking up and down the street and then someone saw me and said every day you are here sitting in the park, what happened? I told her about my situation, and she took me in.*

During the evenings when her father was at work, Olivia would secretly return home. Despite the turmoil Oliva faced she gave birth to a healthy baby boy while a woman in the same ward had a stillborn baby. She found it difficult to understand how this could happen.

The relationship with her father did not mend, but by the time she was seventeen Olivia discovered a path through the ashes that helped her to begin rebuilding her life. In a strange way, the woman she met in the park introduced her to another lady. It was this woman who introduced her to the church, where she remained a member to the present day. Church members played a pivotal role in Olivia's life, providing the support, prayers and guidance she needed to overcome the challenges she faced. The prayers, and study of the Bible with a compassionate woman, touched her deeply. This offered a glimmer of hope, during her time of deep suffering and loneliness.

Even though Olivia's relationship with her father deteriorated, after three years of silence, she chose to forgive him and embarked on a process of seeking restoration. She describes the process of forgiveness as a challenging one, but it eventually brought reconciliation and peace between them. She stated:

I felt that everything had crumbled around me, it was a terrible experience and it pushed me over the edge.

She asked:

How am I going to cope, how am I going to survive? There was no one to help me.

Life as she knew it changed when she made three key decisions. The first was when she decided to return to school and take her examinations. The second was when she made the choice to forgive her father. She said:

I saw him as an enemy, but the Bible says that you have to love your enemies. I was able to recognise that my father had problems, I was able to empathise with him and ask what could have led him to do something as crazy as that.

The third decision came with the realisation that God had called her for a purpose. She made the decision to give her life to the Lord and it changed her perspective and gave her a new direction. Despite many struggles, Olivia found that it was 'divine intervention' that helped her to secure a job, receive training, reaching her goal to eventually become a teacher. During her studies she was poor and had few belongings, she found herself working while studying to make ends meet. Hope was the means by which she achieved beauty. Reflecting on her experience, Olivia found solace and comfort in believing that God provides a way of escape in every trial. In forgiving her father, she learnt a salient lesson of the importance of seeing others through God's eyes because she contended:

God allowed me to forgive and move beyond the pain my father inflicted on me.

Thus, Olivia quoted 1 Corinthians 10:13, which reminded her that she was able to overcome her ordeal.

> There hath no temptation taken you but such as is common to man: but God is faithful, who will not suffer you to be tempted above that ye are able; but will with the temptation also make a way to escape, that ye may be able to bear it.

Olivia views her past as a stepping stone, acknowledging the transformative power of faith, and hope. Her story is a testament to the beauty that emerges from the ashes of life's challenges, shaped by a journey that is an unfolding story.

Reflecting on Olivia's Story

> Forgive and you will be forgiven.
>
> Luke 6:37

As an infant, Olivia had a rocky start. For the first two years of her life, she had a mother who was unable to nurture and care for her due to her mental health problems, resulting in being detained in a mental institution. She spent a significant part of her childhood in a residential setting. These are the most important years in a child's life, but Olivia did not have access to security and missed out on the opportunity to form a significant attachment with her mother during her developmental and most formative years. As a result, the problems her parents experienced led to their separation and a significant loss of security and attachment to them. Olivia had no control over the decisions that were made for her. She felt that her father was a loving man until she found herself pregnant at the age of thirteen. This disrupted her education, left her homeless and alone after she was abandoned by her father with whom she had developed a positive and loving relationship. Her teen pregnancy brought shame on herself and her father. This was another separation for Olivia, that found her on the streets and alone. Spending days in a nearby park and secretly returning to the family home when her father was at work had all the hallmarks of a stressful situation.

In the midst of her dilemma, Olivia was rescued, at a time when she was in an unstable state of mind and making attempts to lose her baby and her life. A rift was created between Olivia and her father that created a wall of silence. Her ashes experience lasted for three years but eventually and with the support of a stranger she was able to make up for the losses she had suffered. She was blessed with a healthy baby boy, who in later years made her feel proud to be his mother. The church played a key role in supporting Olivia and giving her the confidence to make something of her life. She found her life purpose in becoming a teacher and for many years made a significant contribution to the learning of many children and to the church of which she became a member.

In seeing the beauty Olivia can testify to God's goodness as her life was miraculously saved at a time when she least wanted to live. God allowed her to possess a spirit of forgiveness and to mend the bridge that separated herself and her father.

Highlights from Olivia's Story

- Early life experiences such as separation and loss are significant events and may shape a person's life-long experience
- Forgiveness is the only way to heal from the wounds that are inflicted on us
- Shame can destroy, but the will to reform creates a different story
- The ability to accept support helps to ameliorate stress
- Support is a key to finding one's way out of distress.

Food for Thought

Use your journal or the box below to record your thoughts as you reflect on Janine's story.

1) What was the significance of forgiveness for Olivia's ashes experience?
2) Reflect on who needs your forgiveness and how you can mend bridges through your willingness to forgive.
3) How might forgiveness help you to find inner peace?

CHAPTER TWELVE
From Crisis to Recovery

Do not judge me by my success, judge me by how many times I fell down and got back up.

NELSON MANDELA

Each day of our lives presents stresses of one kind or another. There are stressors that come our way from different sources. They may come from the family, an under resourced community, or the work environment in which we are transacting relationships. Work related stress can affect how we function when there are unrealistic expectations, pressure and demands, or power imbalances related to discrimination and institutional oppression. Some stress may be internally generated from personal anxiety and worry, cultural differences, the inability to meet deadlines or even the failure to plan. Stress becomes a crisis when we are unable to establish work/life balance and promote our health. The World Health organisation defines health as:

> a state of complete physical, mental and social wellbeing and not merely the absence of disease or infirmity.

The National Health Service definition of mental health states that:

> Mental health is a state of wellbeing in which the individual realises his or her own abilities, can cope with the normal stresses of life, can work productively and fruitfully and is able to make a contribution to his or her own community.

In order to meet the challenges of life, we must realise that the power to overcome them lies within us. We must also understand how we respond to stressful life events, by examining our behaviour and our responses to stress. Whether stress is short term, such as a having a disagreement or long-term, such as a major upheaval both require an understanding of how the body reacts to stress. Self-awareness is an essential tool for managing stress. To know yourself is to know how your body responds to unfavourable events. Self-awareness also helps in identifying your core values and why they are important to you. As I look back on my career, I can say that my values made all the difference to how I dealt with stress. My values drove the decisions I made because I was willing to stand up for my beliefs. As a leader, I listened to other people's concerns and was able to negotiate and resolve conflict. The ability to resolve internal and external conflict reduces pressure and shifts the balance from illness to wellness. In the next narrative Roseanne became depressed because of family and work-related stress. Her gender, ethnicity and environment were critical stress factors that led to a crisis resulting in mental ill-health.

Roseanne's story

> *I would say that beauty was for me seeing the impossible happen, because I couldn't see anything good coming out of it. It was the seed of the word that caused me to arise.*

Born in Tanzania, Roseanne was the oldest of six children. She was raised in a strict household by parents who were devout Catholics. Growing up she was a shy, quiet introvert, always seeking to please her parents and wanting to meet their expectations. Despite her reserved nature, she developed a reputation as a problem-solver and shone out above her siblings. During her teenage years she projected an image of strength and knew what she wanted to achieve. Her ambition was to become a doctor. Roseanne excelled at school and graduated with an honour's degree at university. She chose medicine as her career and was accepted at medical school.

By the age of twenty-one Roseanne was engaged to a fellow graduate. Her future looked promising. However, her world crumbled when her fiancé broke off their engagement, shattering the life she had envisioned. She chose a faith denomination that her parents did not approve of. Her convictions led to her baptism into the Seventh Day Adventist Church. She was disowned and rejected by her entire family. She felt the weight of her parents' disapproval after they discontinued all contact with her, insisting that she should give up her newfound faith.

Rising above the challenges of a broken relationship and rejection by her parents Roseanne completed her studies and graduated as a doctor. She answered the call to serve as a missionary doctor. Facing the trials of a male-dominated environment she often felt overwhelmed and disheartened. Having lost her family, her homeland and the people that were closest to her, Roseanne struggled to make sense of her life. Some fifteen years later Rosanne did not meet a partner and her wish to have children did not materialise. She was left feeling disillusioned and disappointed.

Seeking a fresh start, Roseanne moved to the United Kingdom, nursing wounds from her past, the loss of her fiancé as well as the loss of her family. Isolation and depression took hold, leading to a nervous breakdown that transformed her from a confident problem-solver to someone grappling with internal chaos and crisis. Having secured a job as a gynaecologist in a teaching hospital, Roseanne felt that she had turned the corner. However, a pivotal moment occurred when her professional integrity was challenged by a male colleague. As she was giving a presentation, memories from her past surged as she was publicly humiliated and criticised. She felt that the unwarranted criticism was located in a gender and racial bias, thereby increasing the intensity of her emotional pain. It was this event, as well as other discriminations and injustices at work, which led her to resign from a job where she was beginning to regain her confidence. Once again Roseanne questioned her ability to manage herself and sank into further depression. She was unable to work and remained at home shut in and isolated from the world. Unable to manage her emotions she fell into a deep depressive state.

Roseanne's journey from the depths of mental illness to recovery took several years. Rebuilding her life required overcoming self-doubt and mental anguish. Her path to recovery involved prayer, scripture memorization and cultivating a positive mental attitude as she began to realise the importance of seeking support. Drawing inspiration from Luke 11:9 encouraged her to ask, seek and knock for answers to her prayers. She states:

I learnt how to trust God and to believe that my prayers would be answered, it was praying that encouraged me to seek and persist.

The turning point came when Roseanne secured a position at a teaching hospital where she excelled and eventually became a leader in her field. In the position of delivering babies in complicated cases, she was able to bring joy to many parents as they held their babies in their arms. She received many letters of grateful thanks for her dedication to her work. Unexpected career opportunities unfolded, allowing her to become a credible leader in the field of medicine as she rose from the crucible of fear and disappointment to success.

This was the moment when her ashes turned to beauty. A time came when Rosanne was able to financially support her siblings and her mother after the death of her father. Of this experience she commented, 'God remains faithful ever.' Her greatest lessons about life were to know her purpose and to honour her calling. She commented:

It makes me wonder about my path and how I had lost so much but knowing God and pursuing my profession even though it was at great cost I learnt how to be of service to God and my fellow human beings. I learnt that in losing I won.

Reflecting on Roseanne's Story

It does not always mean that because people were raised by parents who are educationalist that they are automatically raised to be successful or to be emotionally intelligent (EI). The difference between IQ and EI is that the former is measured by external knowledge. This is how we demonstrate an ability to learn and apply concepts. The latter is rooted in a person's self-awareness and their ability to manage their emotions and the emotions of others.

There are a number of intervening factors that determine who and what we become. The first factor is that to a greater extent we have mental images of ourselves and other people. These images are developed from childhood and reach into our adult lives. Second it is essential to have our needs met. In this way, we come to believe that we are loved and cared for, particularly by our parents and significant others. Third, at a foundational level we begin to develop a sense of security and belonging, we are able to love and allow others to love us. On the other hand, when we are rejected, we develop a negative perception of ourselves and will begin to think that there is something wrong with us. Becker and Phelps (2016) rightly state that if we feel inferior to others it is hard to feel deserving of their love. Thus, when Roseanne's relationship with her fiancé broke down, she was unable to cope with the anxiety and sense of unworthiness it provoked.

Rosanne seemingly had opportunities and gifts that many children do not have, but her parents did not provide her with the right type of support, love and validation she needed. In early life she had the misfortune of losing a partner she thought would become her husband. Broken promises can be just as difficult to accept as no promises at all. She had also suffered misfortune in more than one job and found it difficult to recover from the rejections she had encountered. People can feel jealous when they see that we have gifts and talents that they do not have. They may fail to realise that we all have different gifts and are blessed in different ways. It is jealousy that can in some instances, lead to ill-feelings, discrimination and inequality. Sometimes being a woman in a male-dominated environment can also lead to discriminatory practices.

Without a network of support Roseanne's health declined and she found herself grappling to contain her emotions, and possibly feeling the weight of failure.

Personal Relationship: The Crisis of a Breakdown

Whether the breakdown of a relationship results from family discord, romantic or work-based relationships, they all have the same effect on a person's emotional and psychological wellbeing. They create a negative cycle of thoughts, feelings, sensations and behaviours that entrap and lead to distressing symptoms. Broken relationships invariably result in suffering and can be destructive, as is evident from Rosanne's revelations. Relationships are primarily concerned with satisfying a need for a sense of belonging and connectedness. In this scenario, Rosanne found it difficult to initiate other relationships because of the fear that the same issues would reoccur. This may not be necessarily true, but it was how her thoughts caused her to focus on self-blame and feelings of inadequacy, which in turn made her vulnerable and eventually depressed.

One of the lessons we can learn from Roseanne's story is that her faith was a strong factor in her eventual recovery. She was able to complete her studies during the early life stages even though the relationship she most desired was not fulfilled. However, because she did not have any therapeutic intervention at the time, when similar situations of rejection arose, she was unable to cope and returned to the vicious cycle of being self-deprecating. She had learnt how to be self-critical. On the other hand, her way of escape was to follow her calling and in time it opened the door for her to follow her chosen path and become successful.

A key point in Rosanne's story is that at the time of her broken relationship she made a decision to become a missionary. This action took her away from the problem she was facing and into a male-dominated environment where she did not have the emotional tools to cope with the discrimination she faced. In many ways she felt as if she was stepping out of the sinking boat and stepping on dry land, but it turned out to be the very opposite of what she needed to recover at that time. Her decision-making at the time was a crucial factor in the way she performed.

Significant to moving from ashes to beauty was Rosanne's inner gifts, one of which was the determination to succeed. Her recovery came through a consistent prayer life and taking steps to make the transition that was necessary to move her to the next step. Success for Rosanne was found in using the gift of healing others through her professional expertise to the point where it was recognised and where she was given accolades for her diligence and approach to patient care. It was at this point that she found a true sense of belonging and identity. In reality, she had transitioned from a state of ashes to beauty. It was her inner strength that ultimately gave her the strength to overcome adversity, thus she became a resilient woman. Her ashes turned to beauty when she realised the power of prayer and of dependence on God to bring her through a tumultuous storm in her life.

Highlights from Rosanne's story

- Remember that broken relationships can have a devastating effect on your ability to function
- Broken relationships can lead to a crisis so seek early help
- Learn how to recognise the symptoms of mental ill-health problems
- Mental health issues can have different effects on different people because we are not all the same and our responses to problem-solving can vary
- When you recognise that your functioning is not at an optimum level take steps to self-care and try not to isolate yourself or self-blame
- Search for the needle in the haystack, there is always a glimmer of hope, and you will find it if you seek for it
- Reflect on your thoughts, feelings, sensations and behaviour
- Seek professional help for unresolved emotional issues.

Food for Thought

Use your journal or the box below to complete the following activities.

1) Thinking back to a loss you have experienced as a woman how can you honour your strengths?
2) How can you live in the present and take every moment and make it a force for good?

3) Write down the names of two people in your network that you know you can call on for support when you are feeling anxious or depressed.

Further Food for Thought

We all have times when we feel mentally challenged by the things that happen to us. Identify a time when you felt mentally challenged and what happened before you felt unwell.

1) What were your thoughts?
2) What were your feelings?
3) What sensations did you feel?
4) What behaviours did you notice?
5) Thinking back to that situation what could you have done differently?
6) What actions can you take to help someone who is feeling mentally unwell?

CHAPTER THIRTEEN

The Quest for Beauty

The most beautiful sea hasn't been crossed yet. The most
beautiful child hasn't grown up yet. The most beautiful days we
haven't seen yet. And the most beautiful words I wanted to tell
you haven't been said yet

NAZIM HIKMET

The quest for beauty comes as we are bestowed with it through the
benevolence of God who is gracious and compassionate. If you go in
quest of beauty, you will find it. As Nazim Hikmet, a Turkish poet, reminds
us, beauty has to be discovered. In our finite state we must go in quest of
beauty moving through a difficult process. If you are diligent, you will find
it in nature, the wind, the rain, the snow, the storm, the fire and the ashes.
You will find it in quietness or in turmoil. You will find it in trial, in pain, in
suffering and the testing of your faith relationship with God. You will find
it in music, art, architecture, speech, and hope when there is hopelessness
and helplessness. You will find it in your children, your partner, your
parents, grandparents, in other relatives or your friendship with others
whether at work or in the community where you live. It is possible to find
beauty in the simple yet complex things of life, such as going through a life-
threatening health problem or creating routine to change your diet or
achieve better exercise habits. You can find it in failure and in success, in
sadness and happiness or when you celebrate another person's happiness.
The quest for beauty emerges as a lost pearl of great price and moves beyond
the type of beauty that we naturally gravitate towards.

Some years ago, I visited California and had the privileged of seeing the
giant Sequoia trees, the tallest living species of trees in the world. They were
truly a thing of beauty. I have seen dolphins at San Diego Zoo and was

amazed after I came face to face with the beauty of their intelligence. I have seen a beautiful sunset in the Caribbean and watched with awe as it disappeared past the horizon.

I discovered that the women of this study were motivated to go on a quest for beauty in a number of ways.

1. Service to others: Service to others generally springs from a heart of love and concern. We should not love others for what they are able to gives us, but because we are given an opportunity to show and express the emotion of love in an unconditional way. John 3:16 says: *"For God so loved the world, that he gave his only begotten Son, that whosoever believeth in Him should not perish, but have everlasting life."*
   In him we live, and move and have our being. Acts 17:28. We cannot truly love until we discover the beauty that lies within us and how it motivates us to be of service to others. We are capable of loving others as we seek to understand differences and why they exist. Many years ago, my friend's husband disclosed to me that he grew up in South Africa. As a white privileged male, he did not associate with black people and saw them as inferior. However, one day he was on a boat that capsized and a black man risked his life and saved him from death. It was after this experience that he came to understand the power of service and love.

2. Through passion and purpose: The passion we have comes across as beauty when people see that we are committed and have a purpose beyond self-interest. Passion leads us to do the best we can by developing the confidence to take action and to stand by the principles we believe to be commendable. It helps us to uphold values such as integrity, honesty, truthfulness, self-sacrifice and a non-judgmental attitude. It leads us away from negative thoughts such as jealousy, bigotry, malice, hatred, pride and intentions that are abusive and harmful. Life purpose is the reason for living and interacting with others, it leads us to do great works and to give of ourselves even when we lack courage. My personal passion is to embrace the gifts I have been given and my purpose it to allow others to see what they can

become through the gift of beauty I possess. This has nothing to do with how I look as a person but everything to do with my thoughts and the willingness to be gracious.

3. Through sharing resources: We are all given internal resources that we can share with others. We become beautiful people when we see others in need and reach out to help them. Whether our resources are meagre or plentiful, if we are able to share with those who are less fortunate than us, it makes us beautiful people. In the sharing of our internal resource, the true quest is to communicate a message of acceptance and love.

4. By being kind and compassionate: There are some people who do not know how to be kind, they are absorbed in themselves, they cultivate the character of a narcissist. These are people who are self-centred and who crave attention and admiration. Kindness in all its multifaceted forms causes us to reach out to others, sometimes when it is less expected. Being compassionate calls forth the best in us, shifting how we see those in need leading us to respond to distress. It allows us to sympathise and empathise. The person with empathy sees beauty through the eyes of another person.

5. By showing gratitude: Each day we are alive is a day to show gratitude. A beautiful person searches for different ways to say thank you. We can do it by connecting with others in a way that they did not expect. We can find beauty by expressing positive thoughts. We can search for beauty as we look for ways to show our appreciation. Jesus told a parable about ten lepers whom He had cleansed. This story is told in Luke Chapter 17. The ten lepers met Jesus as he was on his way to Jerusalem on the borders of the two cities. They were outcasts searching for healing. As they approached him, they said have mercy on us, nothing else was important. Jesus responded with compassion. He did not ask if they were Samaritans or Jews and he did not define them by who they were. He told all ten to go to the priest, but before they reached him, they were healed. It was the response of the nine lepers that provoked the question Jesus asked after one returned to give

thanks. He said: "Didn't I heal ten? Where are the other nine? What came to light is that the leper who returned to give thanks got an extra blessing, he received more than physical healing. He received a spiritual blessing because it was his faith that impressed him to glorify God and his thanks that made him fully healed.

6. Through brokenness: Most people would argue that it is difficult to find beauty when their lives are shattered beyond recognition. Separation and loss of many kinds undoubtedly have a devastating impact on human functioning. Losing a loved one, losing one's home or job is highly stressful, and consequently interrupts an otherwise normal flow and orderly routine. Hearing that your child has committed a criminal offence brings brokenness. In order to live through brokenness, it is important to have faith in the eternal God who provides a refuge during the time of storm. The refuge represents a place of safety, it is like an oasis in a barren desert. In the same way that the potter works with clay and mends the cracks in the vessel, so too God works with us, so that we can embrace the beauty of a restored life. God told Jerimiah to go to the potter's house because the vessel he made was blemished so he made another vessel that seemed good to the potter. Jerimiah 8:1-4. Brokenness is not the end, but the beginning of great things.

7. Through knowledge: Education and learning is a game-changer, it moves us to a place where we can embrace knowledge and share it with others. I have been a lecturer and freelance trainer for over forty years. One of my greatest joys has been sharing my knowledge with students, practitioners, parents and learners from all walks of life. The beauty in knowledge is how it enhances our capacity to see learning as a lifelong pursuit. It allows us to not only see the beauty in ourselves but the beauty and potential in others. Not only do others benefit from the knowledge we gain but also from the knowledge we transfer. However, the key is to first go in quest of knowledge through studying, reading, reflection and dialogue.

8. Embracing the quest for change: The person who is seeking change is also seeking beauty, because they want to alter their circumstances

and responses to life's problems. He/she realises that change is consonant with growth. We do not change for the sake of changing, but because it is transformative and rewarding. It brings new experiences as we go along life's journey. A lack of self-confidence may stop us from making the changes that are necessary by placing limitations on our thinking, thus keeping us in a can't do posture. Change that is transformational will substantially impact many areas of your life. For example, I decided that I wanted to change an aspect of my work-life. I made small changes by applying for a job that required different skills. Having completed an application form, I faced the process of attending an interview. The real change came when I was appointed and had to deliver according to the job description. My willingness to make a change not only led to new opportunities but I was encouraged to keep seeking for ways to make improvements and further advancement. One of the best ways to facilitate change is to introduce small incremental modifications. Set routines that become habitual and are part of a new lifestyle. Change also involves letting go of the things we like, but are harmful and challenging ourselves to make a new start.

9. Spiritual connectedness: When we go in quest of spiritual connectedness it aligns our actions with God's purpose so that we can first connect with Him, and then with our fellow human beings. We see the world from a different vantage point, we begin to see what God originally created as beautiful. Spiritual connectedness takes us to the next level, so that we focus on the best, overlooking the flaws we commonly tend to exaggerate in others and at times ourselves. From this spiritual perspective, we are given insight to understand that no one is perfect. We are a work in progress. Jesus had spiritual connectedness with His father because He prayed for oneness or unity with his father and with us. In John 17:20-21 Jesus prayed for unity with the Father. Spiritual connectedness helps us to seek forgiveness and extend it to others. We are beautiful as we recognise that forgiveness first comes from God and as a result, He puts it

within our hearts to forgive as we have been forgiven. Herein lies true spiritual connectedness. The quest for beauty unfolds the mysteries of many spiritual qualities we can possess.

Life is:

> A mystery, Unfold it.
> A journey, Walk it.
> Painful, Endure it.
> Beautiful, See it.
> A joke, Laugh at it.
> A song, Sing it.
> A flower, Smell it.
> Wonderful, Enjoy it.
> A candle, Light it.
> Precious, Don't waste it.
> A gift, Open it.
> Love, Give it.
> Unlimited, Go for it.
> Light, Shine in it.

IYANLA VANZANT

As we move onto the next chapter, I will show how the quest for beauty against a backdrop of ashes and storm was manifested in the lives of each woman I interviewed.

CHAPTER FOURTEEN

Emerging Themes

> The most beautiful people we have known are those who have known defeat, known suffering, known struggle, known loss and have found their way out of the depths. These persons have ... an understanding of life that fills them with compassion ... a deep loving concern. Beautiful people do not just happen.
>
> ELIZABETH KUBLER-ROSS

In analysing the narratives, I found that there were nine strong themes that emerged from the interviews. The first was the prevalence of mental health, the second was loss. The third was the impact of abuse. Fourth was acceptance and restoration, the fith was the significance of social support, the sixth was radical transformation, the seventh was surrender. The eighth finding was the capacity to forgive and the nineth was resilience and self-awareness. Each story was unique and weaved unique elements related to ashes, storm and beauty. It is at this point that I can delve into the key themes and how they emerged.

Mental Health as a Central Theme

Mental health was the strongest theme in all of the stories. These consisted of disorders that could be diagnosed, ranging from anxiety, depression, bipolar, psychosis and post-traumatic stress. Of the ten women, seven reported feeling depressed, three suffered with suicidal thoughts and two actually attempted suicide. Each story portrayed the individuals grappling with a spectrum of mental health disorders that disrupted their normal flow of life and became distressing, clearly involving a change in thinking patterns, actions and behaviour that significantly disrupted their lives. There were a variety of triggers caused by their circumstances including childhood trauma, family problems, relationship breakdowns, workplace stress and societal pressures. Each profoundly affected their ability to function, leading to homelessness, isolation, financial loss and a sense of being trapped in a cycle of fear and despair.

Stigma and Misunderstanding. It is difficult for others to understand the torment that depression can bring and the suffering that a mental health disorder causes because sometimes there is no physical evidence. We cannot see what is going on in a person's head. I found that there was pervasive fear associated with mental health problems. As a result, the participants hid their struggles due to societal misconception and derogatory attitudes toward mental health conditions as well as feelings of shame. This stopped them from speaking out for fear of exposure and ridicule. It was interesting that this small but important study gave the participants an opportunity to speak from their site of pain and points out the need for further research in the context of exchanging ashes and storm for beauty.

Mental health problems had affected them in different ways depending on their ashes experience. What led them into the fire and the storm were circumstances over which they had no control. Each story showed that there was a sense of disappointment, despondency, pervasive fear, feelings of rejection, unhappiness, relationship problems, loss of a relationship and loss of employment. There was also a theme of racism, discrimination, stress and inequality in the work environment that led to depression. The women were tested in many ways and as a result almost came to the end of their limited resources. However, the desire to search for beauty brought a different outcome.

Emotional Impact of Depression

It was revealing that while the participants were not told what to talk about as their ashes or storm experience, ninety percent of the participants talked about their mental health at some level. The ashes and the storm symbolised a roller-coaster of emotions causing profound distress and even leading to suicidal ideation and attempts to end their life or feeling that they were undeserving of the gift of life, or that their lives were not worth living. Despite recounting historical events it was difficult for them to go through the pain of their memories.

Two of the ten suffered with psychosis and one of them was sectioned and detained in a mental health institution. Two had a parent who was detained in hospital, a genetic condition they suffered from in later life. One of the participants was diagnosed as having bipolar. All of the women referred to depression and anxiety as having impacted their general wellbeing and ability to function emotionally. I found that whether their experience could be described as ashes or storm it took them through a roller-coaster experience, and even though they were recalling historical events they were moved to the point of becoming tearful as they recalled the emotional impact of their experiences.

Each narrative included depression. This was a way of describing what they termed 'dark moods', crying, feeling helpless, being hopeless and feeling an intense sense of being alone and in a dark place. It included feeling hopeless, wanting to end their life, and feeling that they did not deserve to live. In the cases of Sally, Janine and Olivia, the disorders were so acute that they wanted to die. In the cases of Jamila, Davina and Maranda their feelings of depression were created by others while Sally had long-standing and deep-rooted family dysfunctional problems that stemmed from childhood and merged into her adult life with memories of anger and bitterness. On the other hand, Clarissa's attack of burnout was sudden and was related to stress, yet she found herself cut off from others and unable to stand up. Amina's, Maranda's and Roseanne's depression was related to unexpected relationship breakdowns that had a devastating impact on them and their coping abilities, which were seriously reduced. Trudy had childhood depression related to being bullied and treated as an outcast after a life-altering accident. She also had to cope with the loss of her parents during her childhood. In the case of Olivia, it was separation from her mother, and later her father that brought on depression leading her to feel like an outcast. The separation of her parents led to an experience of being in the public care system, teen pregnancy and abandonment. It was the teen pregnancy that finally led to shame, and disgrace. She not only wanted to end her life, but the life of her unborn child, while Janine felt as if she would not have the capacity to love her unborn child. Each episode in their lives had an impact on their mental functioning. Olivia exclaimed that the experience of depression was like 'walking in a dead man's shoes.' Roseanne appeared to be an unlikely case, but mental health is not dependent on status or education. What led to her depression was the rejection she felt after the breakdown of a relationship she thought would last, and male domination in the workplace; rejection of her parents associated with her religious choice was also a strong factor leading to her illness.

A similar story emerged for Maranda's and Amina's stories after their relationships failed and threw them into the world of single parenthood. They both suffered financial loss, taking them to the brink and leading them into physical and mental illness. The study showed that loss can take many forms and financial misfortune and bankruptcy caused directly by others emerged as a significant loss. The emotional toll of mental health disorders is profound, often hidden beneath the surface. The narratives disclosed feelings of torment, helplessness, loneliness and shame, highlighting the unseen burden of psychological pain and suffering. In her book *Shame: Resiliency Theory* Brené Brown (2015) draws attention to the phenomenon of shame which has a way of causing us to lose our authenticity. She argues that it 'derives its power from being unspeakable' because it makes us feel vulnerable. The table on the following page shows the risk factors associated with mental ill-health, the common emotional responses to it and the factors that lead to resilience.

Risk Factors	Emotional Responses	Resiliency Factors
Separation, Loss and Trauma	Sadness, Unresolved Grief	Independence
Depression	Neglecting Self-care	Looking Forward
Anger and Anxiety	Isolate and Self-blame	Social Support
Fear and Self-doubt	Hopelessness	Hopefulness
Feeling Rejected	Stressed	Building New Relationships
Feeling Shame – Unworthy	Negative Thought Processes	Worthy – New Mindset
Loneliness	Separate from others	Liberated To Take Control
Brokenness	Bitterness, Regret	Mending The Broken Pieces
Silence	Withdrawal of Speech	Creating A Voice
Shame	Paranoia	Seek Social Support
Racism/Discrimination	Excluded/Stereotyped	Self-belief & Collective Responses

Loss

The theme of loss was consistently repeated in each of the narratives and provided a link with feelings of hopelessness. It was one of the factors that led to depression. After loss a person experiences grief, which may not be recognised as such. Loss can happen in many different ways and is associated with ashes, because it may feel like death and the stripping away of someone or something that a person gives significant meaning to. It could also be an important attachment that at one time held deep meaning. Loss encompasses bereavement, grief and mourning. However, we seldom associate losing a job, a home or going through a divorce with bereavement and grief. The narratives showed that the timing of the loss, when it began, the number of incidents that occurred and the emotions that it evoked was what led to trauma. Rising out of the ashes depended on the level of support that was available and the ability of the individual to talk to others about their feelings. Additionally, when there was shame, it inhibited their ability to openly express their emotions. The inability to recognise the signs and symptoms of depression and their root cause was identified as a significant factor.

Since loss leads to grief it is critical to be able to find people and or services that can provide help. There was evidence to show that the women sought support in different ways. Some of it came from professionals and some from family and friends. Having access to counselling or life coaching is one way to begin the healing process but a change in thinking and behaviour also helps the grieving process. Grieving allows for acceptance and hence resolution of emotional pain and suffering. It helps with the process of moving on and finding peace. The reality is that as human beings we suffer with multiple losses across the lifespan but when the loss outstrips our coping capacity, it can have a devastating impact on our health and thus, our ability to function. The table below shows the extent to which loss was recurrent across the responses that were given.

Participant	Loss and grief leading to depression	Overcoming grief
Trudy	Loss of parents and sibling, wanted to die	Developed a strong voice
Sally	Loss of nurturing parents, saw her life as meaningless and wanted to die	Used creative skills to rebuild and restructure
Jamila	Loss of a job, finances and livelihood leading to depression	Chose to use creative skills
Amina	Loss of home, business, finances, divorce, loss of self-confidence	Focused on education and achievement
Maranda	Loss of home and possessions, finances, loss of relationship	Focused on becoming independent and praying
Janine	Loss of opportunity to study, became depressed and suicidal	Made life-style changes
Olivia	Loss of a significant relationship, became suicidal	Returned to education and focused on being a good parent
Clarissa	Loss of mental faculty	Focused on praying
Davina	Loss of opportunity for promotion	Made the decision to move on
Roseanne	Separation from parents and loss of a significant relationship	Focused on her career

Abuse

Most of the narratives had an underlying, but at times clear theme of abuse. The abuse was perpetrated by individuals and institutions. There are specific definitions of abuse provided by the Department of Health (DH2000). Abuse occurs when a person is deemed to be vulnerable and unable to protect themselves against significant harm or exploitation. It is characterised as:

> When someone misuses their power or control over another person, causing harm or distress. The abuser could be in a close relationship with the adult at risk. They could be someone the adult at risk depends on and trusts.
>
> DEPARTMENT OF HEALTH

Abuse takes different forms and are defined by the Department of Health as:

> Physical, sexual, psychological, financial, material, neglect, acts of omission, discrimination or institutional abuse.

Each type of abuse is a violation of a person's human rights, resulting in fear, intimidation and silence. In a marriage relationship domestic abuse encompasses each of the definitions provided above and can result in disfigurement or death. Amina and Maranda spoke of psychological and verbal aggression as well as financial exploitation leading to the loss of their homes. When Olivia was abandoned as a child, she was also abused because she was deprived of shelter and emotional warmth. Institutional abuse occurred in the story of Jamila who was unfairly dismissed from her job, and was made to sign a document prohibiting her from later making a claim for compensation. She was excluded, humiliated and made to feel different on the basis of her skin colour resulting in unfair bias. While being over-qualified Davina was denied promotion. Roseanne suffered racial and gender abuse in more than one institution, making her feel unwelcomed and undervalued. Trudy suffered cruelty and bullying that reduced her to a state of persona non grata. It is usually the shame and the silence that allows abuse to flourish and the perpetrator to hold power over the victim.

Verbal abuse is psychologically and emotionally damaging because it results in a loss of confidence. The threats that accompany verbal abuse induces fear through coercion leading to a loss of personhood.

Acceptance and Restoration

I found that an important link between the narratives was acceptance and restoration. Each of the women demonstrated vividly that the notion of acceptance and restoration is the path to healing. People cannot truly heal unless they realise that healing comes from within. Acceptance may not appear to be the best way to set out on the path of wellness because it is a battle and a challenge to accept misfortune. Yet, the dilemma is that acceptance allows progress to take place.

Even though the women had gone through traumatic experiences they learnt that the only way to find peace was to seek healthy responses to the ashes and the storm. In order to start thinking in a new way, they had to adopt a new perspective on life by accommodating change. The strategies they used included praying and extending faith in a benevolent God. Those who did not profess to be Christians nevertheless made reference to praying as a powerful tool that led to restoration of health and wellbeing. Although at the time the women were not initially able to accept what had happened to them, when they did, restoration came with the realisation that their emotions could not be smothered or extinguished. A restored life would only come as they adopted healthy coping strategies, which led them to understand that challenges are the testing ground for growth.

Taking into account the stories, one would think that acceptance would be difficult to do, but the juxtaposition is to be found in the search for healing. Therefore, in seeking the answer to acceptance, I discovered that it is a state of mind and one that bridges the gap between the need to hold on to negative experiences and the desire to heal. The latter is the stronger because it caused the women to look beyond the underlying reasons for what happened to them and to a brighter future. With self-acceptance comes internal resources to take the long road to recovery. This meant going through a process; even though I found that the process was incredibly difficult, it produced lasting change as was evidenced in each one of the stories that were recounted. To be restored requires support and self-care. This theme of acceptance could be likened to the fifth stage of dying defined by Kubler-Ross.

Kubler-Ross (1970) stated that reaching the end of life is the fifth stage. which she calls "Acceptance"; at this time a person "wants to be strong, but seeks solace and strength from the scriptures to accept whatever may come." We can see this resolve to move on and accept whatever life brings reflected in the women's stories. They had progressed through previous stages and now they had reached the point of acceptance and renewal.

Social Support

Support made all the difference to recovery. Support is predicated on the notion of rebuilding inner resources through a process that bridges the gap between independence and interdependence. During times of stress and life challenges it is social support that leads to recovery. Psychologists and mental health professionals have found that social support can help people to overcome some of the most difficult emotional problems when there is a solid support network. They argue that strong social support promotes wellness while poor social support is often linked with depression and suicide (American Psychological Association, 2022). It builds on relationships and creates stronger connections with family, friends and significant others and is a buffer against the onslaught of negative experiences. When emotional support is available it also proves to be a protective factor against loneliness and other long-term health conditions.

Support allows people to overcome mental health problems which can be soul-destroying. Thus, Jamila recalled that after facing discrimination at work she was able to rebuild her life through the support of family and friends. Clarissa pointed to her mother's support as the key to her survival, as did Jamila, Davina and Maranda, all found support to be the key to recovery. Each one of the women acknowledged that support helped them on the road to recovery.

There are a number of benefits that are derived from social support, among them are improved quality of life and helping people to stay socially connected. Taylor (2011) identified psychological, emotional and physical types of support that help to reduce stressful conditions. In actuality, social support promotes survival, consequently the more support that is provided the better able we are to fight off and cope with trauma and other life events that lead to poor health.

If we think of the Covid-19 pandemic and how people suffered as a result of a lack of social support and connections, we know that it had a detrimental and sustained effect on people's ability to connect with each other. The inability to physically see, touch, hug or kiss those who were closest to us had far-reaching implications for mental health both in adults and children, because a real wall was created that shut off vital types of support from family, friends and community services. Once restrictions relaxed people could only see those within their bubble, and it continued to restrict connections that they might have otherwise had with fictive kin, which is to say, people who are not blood relatives.

The health encyclopaedia points to the power of social support. It helps people to make relationships stronger by using modern-day technological systems that enable them to meet on a regular basis. It was during the pandemic that Trudy was able to provide support to vulnerable people for whom support was a key measure. Support is inexorably linked to comfort. It was interesting to see that when comfort was given it eventually resulted in a pathway to giving comfort to others. The idea of giving back was ably demonstrated in each of the narratives and showed the extent of their gratitude. It is important to remember that Christ comforts us in our distress.

On the other hand, the absence of support can lead to a downward spiral. There were those who lacked support and this had an impact on their ability to cope as it intensified feelings of loneliness. I found that there was lack of support in Maranda, Amina and Janine's narratives. However, the turning point to restoration was the effort they had put into finding a solution that worked for them. Olivia lost the support of her father after she was abandoned but the friendship of a stranger helped to ameliorate her deep loss. Equally, I found that when friends reinforced the women's creativity and ability to succeed, they were able to turn around what appeared to be a hopeless situation into a hopeful one.

Radical Transformation

> And be not be conformed to this world; but be ye transformed by the renewing of your mind, that ye may prove what is that good and perfect will of God.
>
> Romans 12:2

Transformation must first begin in the mind because this is where we learn how to create a new story. Transforming from the ashes or from the storm was a colossal task for each of the women in this research. I found that transformation was critical to their recovery, but it took time and occurred at different stages, and required them to adopt the mindset of change. It was after Trudy recognised that the loss of her parents and brother produced a different type of knowledge, namely self-knowledge, that she embarked on a process of change. She stopped looking at the physical scars and shifted her attention away from endless makeovers to inner beauty. As difficult as it was to progress through the stages of bereavement, she recognised the need to help others and in so doing she was transformed. It was only after Jamila recognised that she was an outsider that she changed her thought processes and began to look for new opportunities. The same was true for Davina, because she resolved to look for an open door and in so doing transformed her work opportunities and life chances. Maranda changed her life chances when she made the decision to end her marriage after her husband's infidelity and abuse. In so doing she developed the latent talents that were available to her. Finding independence was also crucial to her personal development. Amina and Clarissa took a transformational step by holding on to the ideal that they wanted to change their lives through academic studies. Janine fought against the real problem of mental decline and rose out of the ashes, gaining considerable satisfaction from her work with mentally ill people. Roseanne became successful after she relied on God and his power to sustain her during the dark and lonely days.

By way of comparison some of the women rose out of the ashes through creativity; Sally, Maranda and Jamila provided the best examples of creativity while going through the ashes. Each story holds this very important concept of transformation. Transformation came with discernment and the intention to seek wisdom. The Bible says:

> If any of you lack wisdom, let him ask God that giveth to all men liberally, and upbraideth not; and it shall be given to him. But let him ask in faith, nothing wavering. For he that wavereth is like a wave of the sea driven with the wind and tossed.
>
> James 1: 5-8

Transformation produces evidence that we are no longer the same, we are not tossed about in the sea of destruction, but we are set on a new course. In order to make the transition from a caterpillar to a butterfly the change must involve an upward spiral.

There are three discrete stages that ultimately led to radical transformation.

Introspection: During this stage there was resistance to accepting their situations; nevertheless, it led to critical introspection. They asked questions such as, why did this happen to me? Why me and not someone else? And why do I have to suffer? The answer was hidden much like the hidden pearl in the oyster. Undoubtedly, suffering has a purpose and is part of the process of growing. They came to accept that life does not choose its victims, but life happens. Introspection helped the women to better understand themselves in relation to others. Their responses were to reach out and help others, in so doing they helped themselves.

Intense emotions: Intense emotions were associated with depression, anxiety, low spirits, self-doubt, feeling isolated, low self-worth, anger, fear and insomnia. These types of emotions were evident in the ten accounts that were given. Radical transformation did not come until they reached a stage of acceptance. This was a very important part of the process because it brought light into a dark world, and it began the process of action-oriented steps to bring about change. The emotion of fear was a strong finding in this study since even the act of contemplating change was threatening. Yet, the only way to conquer the ashes and the storm was to find a way to overcome the emotions that held each of the women in a vice grip of fear.

Surrender: The final stage of radical change involved surrender. Surrendering was a critical aspect of a problem-solution focus, but it also led to commitment to change. For most of the women it was their ability to resort to creating new opportunities, learning new skills, helping others, developing new forms of knowledge, making transitions and moving from where they were to where they would eventually find a resting place. This takes on the analogy of homing pigeons. They set out for a destination but at some point, they are forced to find their way back home. The analysis of the data showed that while each of the women were on a journey, none of it was what they would have chosen. Consequently, they had no idea where it would end. In this context, surrender was what led them to their destination. Thus, a surrendered life became a powerful life. During times of fear and despondency the choice was made to live rather than die, to make a new start rather than succumb to fear, to seek solutions rather than lose hope, to be of service rather than decline into self-pity. Surrendering meant making the choice to come under God's control and governance.

Forgiveness

An aspect of surrender is to forgive and let go. Although Olivia spoke of the pain of abandonment by her father, she found that forgiveness brought change and hence contributed to the process of healing. By letting go of negative emotions associated with a relationship breakdown, she was able to show empathy. Similarly, Clarissa chose to forgive those who misunderstood her condition and were critical rather than compassionate. In order to forgive, Sally's anger against her parents, and in particular her father, brought immense pain and suffering, nevertheless she was able to establish a new relationship with them. Forgiveness involved compassion and insight. Maranda had to let go of animosity and bitter feelings after her husband had ruined her life.

As I reflected on each of the women's stories it became evident that forgiveness was at the heart of the transformation they achieved. Forgiveness is closely aligned with empathy and seeing the world through another person's lens. Forgiveness has an upward spiral that begins with love, positive expression of emotions and communication. Each of these steps reduced inner turmoil as the women exchanged ashes for beauty. I have often heard it said that it is easy to forgive but not to forget, but God says that He will have compassion on us, He will cast our sins in the depths of the sea and remember them no more. Micah 7:19.

Desmond and Mpho Tutu said that *'forgiveness opens the door to peace between people and opens the space for peace within each person.'* This is a perspective that we often fail to realise, particularly when we are struggling with negative emotions such as hate, withholding speech and ignoring those who have done wrong to us. Learning to forgive is one of life's hardest lessons.

There are several benefits to forgiveness. The most integral finding was the implications for a person's health and wellbeing, because forgiveness brings inner peace. As we begin to talk and listen in an empathic way it enhances our ability to understand another person's needs and walk in another person's shoes.

The study showed that forgiveness changes the dynamics of a relationship, particularly if we can acknowledge our wrongdoing and ask for forgiveness. This dynamic of forgiveness changes when people take positions and become unrelenting, thinking that they are right, and the other person is wrong. This type of positioning can and does increase the pain as we seek to shift the blame from ourselves onto others. Forgiveness is an important step in conflict resolution.

Relationships are part and parcel of how we become fulfilled and connected with others. When relationships break down it has a powerful impact on how we feel. It can create fear, uncertainty, sadness, loneliness and a sense of rejection, as was shown in several of the narratives. If there is a financial loss, it has a devastating impact on a person's livelihood, future goals and aspirations. Falsehood and unfaithfulness led to the breakdown of trust making it difficult to recover or reconcile, but the ability to forgive was the only way to find peace.

A key theme that emerged out of this study showed that dishonesty, falsehood and unfaithfulness made forgiveness more difficult to envisage, yet it was possible to do so. This is why the narratives provided a strong emphasis on the theme of forgiveness after a relationship had ended, because it helped the recovery process. Kushner (1981) in his book entitled, When Bad Things Happen to Good People, maintains that *'the ability to forgive and the ability to love are the weapons God has given us to help us live fully.'*

Thus, forgiveness opens the door to reconciliation and reconstructing a new relationship. Although a relationship may not be exactly the same as it was, we can find a way to let go of negative feelings. I found that forgiveness by choice was clearly seen in Jamila's narrative where she made a determined effort to change her perception of the harm that others had inflicted on her.

When seen as a choice, forgiveness urges us to let go and move forward. Choosing to love rather than hate opens the flood gates and allows the light to come in. On the one hand a person who might say that they had forgiven but continue to harbour negative feelings will not experience inner peace. This is not true forgiveness; rather it is when we seek to achieve lasting peace and inner harmony. Roseanne's and Amina's narratives demonstrated that they made a deliberate choice to forgive their parents. This way of acting eventually led to internal healing to the point where they were able to mend broken relationships. I also found that through her ability to forgive Amina made a conscious decision to support her parents after they separated. A similar idea is present in Maranda's journey when she chose to find personal independence and let go of bitterness. She was able to move on from a toxic relationship; it was a decision that supported her mental health and general wellbeing.

Forgiveness places emphasis on our strength because it defines our character and identity. The person who is able to show strength through trial motivates others to find a way out of any impasse. The strength we bring resides within us and is related to our own experiences and how we deal with setbacks and disappointments. Examples of strength of character were found across the narratives.

Forgiveness makes us emotionally intelligent in that it helps us to regulate and modulate some of the strongest impulses we have learnt. Emotional intelligence makes us self-aware; it gives us the ability to manage our own emotions and it helps us to understand the emotions of others and to manage our every-day relationships. It is a form of otherness that creates a balance between what we feel for ourselves and what we feel for others. Even though the path to forgiveness is not an easy one, it draws attention to ourselves and how weak and frail we can become. It encourages us to 'walk through the shoals of hatred, anger, and make our way through grief and loss to find the acceptance that is the hallmark of forgiveness' (Desmond and Mpho Tutu). Essentially it is looking at the life of Christ and understanding how his emotional intelligence allowed Him to bear the sting of rejection and to forgive those who were His staunchest enemies. In this He boldly said, 'Father, forgive them, for they know not what they do.' Luke 23:34.

Forgiveness served as a bridge to healing, allowing the women to unburden themselves from the weight of the past to find a measure of consolation in the present. The tool of prayer became the key factor in bringing healing by letting go of bitterness, anguish, and resentment. Such phrases as 'I fell on my face and prayed', 'prayer became my salvation', 'prayer was believing that God would provide for my needs', 'I trusted that God would answer my prayer' and 'my mum was a praying woman', were testament to their faith. Therefore, prayer was found to be a dimension of forgiveness because it allowed the women to become hopeful.

Resilience and Self-Awareness

> Resilience is the process of adapting well in the face of adversity, trauma, tragedy, threats or significant sources of stress, such as family and relationship problems or workplace and financial stressors.
>
> AMERICAN PSYCHOLOGICAL ASSOCIATION

The emergence of resilience in each of the narratives showed that it is consonant with the definition given by the American Psychological Association. Each of the women had faced traumatic life event, but reached the point of resilience, and this is well-reflected in their stories. As they reflected on their experiences it became clear that they had overcome in ways that might have been impossible if they had not moved from the stage of ashes and storm to beauty. They were survivors.

Although researchers have supported the notion that resilience is about bouncing back, from a Christian perspective it involves much more, it is essentially how we develop trust, faith and hope. It is about how people are able to establish and sustain connected relationships, make good health choices and find their life purpose or true calling. These factors are evident in each of the narratives.

There were experiences of loneliness, domestic abuse, financial hardship, exploitation, discrimination, loss of livelihood, separation, and homelessness which emphasised the theme of brokenness. The challenges of single parenthood added complexity to distress. These were the ashes from which the women had to rebuild their broken lives.

In comparing the narratives, there were unique challenges each woman faced while highlighting the shared theme of navigating adversity and rising from the ashes of life-altering experiences. There were more similarities than differences, but what was different was the actual experience, the context of their problems and their responses to problem-solving. A difference was the cultural background from which the women originated. This reinforces the idea that suffering is a human problem and resilience is the response to overcoming adversity.

The concept of resilience is not new and has been evident in the experiences of oppressed people and communities over many generations where liberation against oppression was the only way of escape. Resilience is sometimes referred to as a strengths-based perspective, connected to the concept of adaptation after a stressful life event or traumatic experience. It is also connected to risk factors associated with one's living environment, which represents the home, the family, the community or one's work environment. There are a number of definitions that theorists have used to define resilience. One of them is:

> … a dynamic process encompassing positive adaptation within the context of significant adversity.
>
> LUTHAR et al. 2000

Some of the historic studies show that resilience is:

> The capacity to maintain feelings of personal integration and sense of competence when confronted by particular adversity.
>
> COHLER 1987

A factor that supported resilience was the ability to recognise and maximise their inner strength and potential. As a result of moving on, through acceptance they were led to go further and create new opportunities. They ultimately cultivated the capacity to emerge feeling encouraged. In so doing, they adapted successfully and were able to give encouragement to others. Attention is drawn to this aspect of resilience in the research of Ledesma (2014) and Southwick et al. (2014). They agree that resilience, though complex, can have different meanings for different people and at different times. We can be more or less resilient in some aspects of our lives. Thus, we can conclude that the women did not reach a stage of perfection but that the area of their lives presented in this study had changed for the better.

All of the women demonstrated different spectrums of creativity. It was noted through the narratives that each of them gained insight or insight was given to them through their spiritual relationship with God and connected relationships with others. It materialised that hope was the link between the narratives because it played a crucial role in the process of emerging from the ashes or the storm and became a guiding light. Current circumstances, no matter how difficult, are not the final chapter. It was faith that made the difference. Despite the odds there existed the potential for a brighter tomorrow. Hope was the catalyst for resilience. It was an inner flame that refused to be extinguished even in the bleakest moments. This is where ashes and storms were traded for a crown of beauty.

The ability to adapt is what helps a person to become resilient. We are all born with the capacity to become strong, but it only becomes evident when we experience setbacks and hurdles. People learn how to become resilient as they face challenging life events, often produced by stress which has a negative impact on a person's ability to function. This is when new opportunities appear on the horizon. Much depends on the type and quality of support that we receive and whether we have the insight to accept support. This type of support often comes from family, friends, identifying with a church, community group or a voluntary group supporting people with similar experiences. Suffering in one domain of our lives can force us to take support from another domain. For example, if a person is affected emotionally and psychologically by a relationship breakdown, turning to family, friends or colleagues can provide the support they need to overcome feelings of anxiety, low morale, lack of confidence, apathy or failure. Equally connected relationships offset loneliness and support self-care.

As we go through various types of hardships, the need to adapt positively leads to re-establishing equilibrium. The question is why some people are able to recover and others are unable to do so. The answer to this question lies in the fact that resilience is a combination of external and internal resources and the confluence of one on the other. The environment and the context of a person's experience are both important in how they make the transition from disappointment to successful recovery. Masten et al. (1990) showed that resilience is the ability to use both internal and external resources successfully. This is the point at which good communication and problem-solving skills are essential. People who are resilient show perseverance under fire, by holding on vigorously and refusing to give up, they achieve it by resting on God's promises. A promise such as Isaiah 41:10 provides comfort and reassurance that we are not alone.

> Fear not I am with thee; do not be dismayed, for I am your God:
> I will strengthen thee, yea, I will help thee, yea I will uphold
> thee: with the right hand of my righteousness.
>
> Isaiah 41:10

Those who sink under pressure are unable to fight back against the storms of life. They find it more difficult to cope with challenges and resort to methods for managing stress and pressure that are not effective in harnessing their inner resources. Their assets are not utilised, and thus, do not work well to their benefit and eventually produce negative outcomes. The challenges they face are not turned into opportunities for growth and transition but missed opportunities because they lack persistence and give up easily.

Resilience is built as we realise that not all events are bad, some of them can lead to better functioning and even transformation in the face of adversity. In order to become resilient, a measure of autonomy is required to begin making self-directed decisions and to act independently of others.

Autonomy is a powerful way to gauge one's sense of purpose and to achieve goals through the process of motivation. Autonomy leads to resilience since it promotes independence. The person who is motivated to survive will do what it takes to find a solution through problem-solving. In other words, resilience helps us to be solution-focused. It means taking control of one's circumstances and refusing to give in or give up. It is an important step in finding one's true identity and knowing one's life purpose.

The resilient person will not only take personal control, but they will seek help and support when they recognise that no one is an island. We all need others to help us in the struggle to find solutions to our problems.

Autonomy is also connected to spiritual growth because our faith makes us more determined and is a protective factor. Faith is the key that opens the door to new opportunities. When people find their personal autonomy, they also become successful at managing strong and sometimes contradictory emotions.

We are most likely to become resilient when we take advantage of protective factors that exist in the environment in which we are operating. These are commonly contained within supportive relationships, building positive energy within relationships and social competence, namely the ability to perform at a level where we can interact positively with others.

In the face of adversity, I found that the women demonstrated the ability to become socially competent. Social competence occurs when people develop the ability to move on from negative experiences. It may mean beginning again or fighting back and restructuring to win the battle against the odds. Resilient people tend to be flexible; they are empathic and develop a sense of the need to weave their way out of adversity. They tend to be resourceful, creative and reflective. Resilience shows up when there are high expectations even when we are at the lowest points of our lives.

The beauty appears after we have fought against the vicissitudes of life and lead us to move forward, finding new vistas. It takes a diligent type of searching to move from the ashes to find one's true self and true internal beauty. God's promises are based on His word and are true. He has told us that while we are yet praying, He will hear (Isaiah 65:24). He has promised to love us so that when we feel unloved, rejected, alone or helpless, He will care for us with an unfailing and immeasurable love. He has promised us His strength and will bear our burdens. If we wait patiently on Him, He will renew our strength, we will mount up on wings like eagles, we will run and not be weary, walk and not faint (Isaiah 40:31). Resilient people are able to use social support systems to build up their internal resources, the strongest of which is faith and a deep belief that God will grant them the desires of their heart.

The women whose lives I portrayed in this book experienced incredible pain and suffering. They survived the ashes and the storm because God strengthened them and made something beautiful out of their lives. Gloria Gaither, the song writer, puts it this way:

"Something beautiful, something good.
All of my confusion He understood.
All I had to offer him was brokenness and strife,
But he made something beautiful of my life."

GAITHER 1971

The transforming grace of God brought about this change in their lives. He turned their ashes and storms into beauty, through their faith.

Looking unto Jesus the author and finisher of our faith; who for the joy that was set before him endured the cross, despising the shame, and is set down at the right hand of the throne of God.

Hebrews 12:2

We too will receive the gift of beauty at the end of our journey.

Self-Awareness

The study found that self-awareness was a key factor in overcoming adversity. It was also interesting, that the women could not become self-aware until they had gone through the process of life-altering events. As a result of their experiences, they had learnt how to look at life from a different vantage point, and in so doing they had mastered the art of self-awareness. They had not only gained an appreciation for their strengths and abilities, but moreover, they learnt how to support others to appreciate what was good about themselves. Thus, helping others meant finding a worthy cause where they could improve their life circumstances by giving back and contributing to the welfare of others. They made choices that were based on self-improvement and advancement. The building blocks of self-awareness was rooted in emotional intelligence and knowing how to express their emotions. In order to become self-aware, we must turn the spotlight inward. One of the first questions we must ask is who am I? The assumption is made that once we know what is on the inside, we will begin to unravel how to respond to negative experiences. It is not what others think of us, but more importantly what we think of ourselves.

Facing Life's Challenges

As human beings we tend to expect that our lives should run smoothly, we do not want to face pain, whether emotionally, physically, spiritually or psychologically. Therefore, the challenges that come as a result of suffering are difficult to tolerate. Yet, challenges provide opportunities for transformation and resilience. They help us to grow and mature into people with experiences that we can share with others as they go through the valley of despair. We must first learn how to deal with personal challenges by turning them into opportunities before we can help others. As we face challenges the most important answer is learning how to persevere and not give up as we go through times of severe testing. Challenges are a part of life, but they can lead to better prospects and eventually to resilience. Giving up serves no good purpose because it does not teach us lessons from which to learn and develop.

We often complain about the valley experiences without realising that the valley produces patience, hope and endurance. We complain about the rain without realising that the sun will break through the clouds. We struggle with why we suffer without realising that if God does not deliver us in the fire or the storm, He will deliver us through them. We may ask how can I be grateful for the things that feel like a crushing weight, without realising that as we are crushed, we are also restored. We are desperate to find a way out of pain, and ill health, yet there is one who is able to comfort us during our hour of need, He stays with us, He has compassion on us and He never leaves or forsakes us. Out of the ashes comes an unusual form of maturity, each trial produces personal growth for which we must give thanks. Gratitude causes people to recognise that life is full of hazards and risks, yet they are able to give thanks for being alive to face another day and another challenge. Being grateful encourages a positive mental attitude, which is a much sought after jewel during times of adversity and the quest for beauty.

Despite facing overwhelming challenges, the participants demonstrated perseverance. Their narratives suggested that as they moved through setbacks and obstacles, they nevertheless held on tenaciously and strove to overcome some of the most life-threatening problems imaginable. Under the stress of depression some of them wanted to end their lives seeing it as meaningless. Essentially, overcoming their problems by persevering eventually led them to find renewal of inner strength.

Discovering the strength they possessed, only became evident after they had gone through the ashes and the storm. Learning how to overcome was of pivotal importance. This was the method by which the women found escape routes to overcome the challenges and find freedom. It was during and after recovery that the recognition of their passion, and the ability to move beyond the crucible of suffering helped them to reach the lighthouse. Gaining insight into their strengths spurred them on to engage in meaningful pursuits, such as helping others, finding a new purpose in life, creative activities, making health changes, embarking on a different journey to achieve independence and moving away from chaotic and dysfunctional relationships. They also discovered that healing came through forgiveness. It was a transformative force. The act of forgiving, whether themselves or those who contributed to their suffering, became a balm for their souls. Forgiveness was a conscious choice and a transformative force that released the shackles of resentment, hatred and fear, welcoming in peace amid inner turmoil.

Internal and external resources are required in our quest for survival when we are going through life's challenges. Different types of resources must be activated as we go through experiences that feel like a passage through ashes or a storm. We are all born as social beings and need others to support and help us make positive and worthwhile connections. Without these connections we become disconnected through isolation and loneliness. There are good reasons for the socialization process which begins from birth and moves through every life stage, ending with death. No man

CRCLE OF LFE: A GRAPHC SUMMARY OF NTERNAL & EXTERNAL RESOURCES

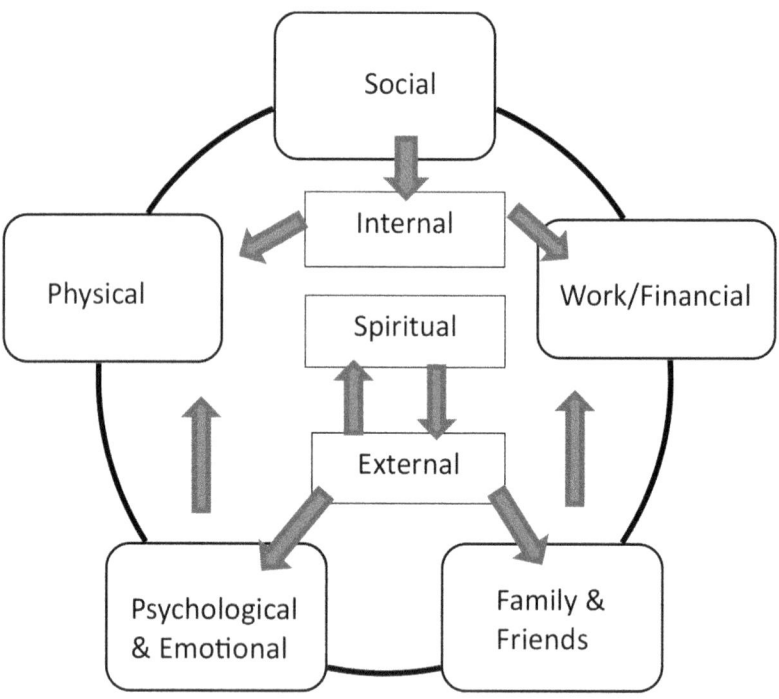

is an island; therefore, it is impossible for us to make it alone. The physical aspects of our existence are personal because we are all different, but generally each life domain whether physical, social, emotional, spiritual or psychological allow us to grow through difficult and troubling times. As the songwriter André Crouch wrote '… *if I didn't have a problem I wouldn't know that God could solve them* …' It is only by going through problems that we are able to rise from the ashes and the storm.

We can become stronger, more effective and more competent if we routinely care for our bodies through daily exercise, fresh air, plenty of water, nutritious meals, adequate sleep and temperance in all things. When challenges come, our resources naturally become depleted, but if we have built strong relationships with family and friends, an enhanced chance of surviving traumatic events that inevitably threaten the very fabric of life is created. Employment aids survival, because it provides the finances we need to meet our responsibilities and needs. If and when there is a lack of financial resources, it can have ramifications of major proportions. The inability to provide for our families can lead to stress and overwhelm. This is why employment is so important, but even in the work environment we can face disappointments that can have a disturbing effect on our psychological and emotional wellbeing.

Spiritual Connectedness

> I praise you because I am fearfully and wonderfully made; your works are wonderful; I know that full well. My frame was not hidden from you when I was made in the secret place, when I was woven together in the depths of the earth.
>
> Psalms 139:14-16

To be spiritually connected is to rely on God who breathed life into our bodies and made us living beings. He is responsible for all things animate and inanimate. It is this entity that supports our internal resources and gives us the determination to shift our thought processes, and emotions so that we can become spiritually well. The spiritual element as an internal resource buffers stress and the pressure that can cause us to lose hope, give up and feel a sense of disillusionment. Integral to internal resources is the trust and hope we exercise to look for a better day. It helps us to remember that God has not given us the spirit of fear but a sound mind, that He gives us the help that is needed to make the most difficult problem feel manageable. We can find a sense of belonging, love and acceptance knowing that His presence is always with us. His grace is sufficient as we go through the fire and storm.

Internal resources are what help us to overcome the psychological dysfunction and emotional turmoil that are inevitably associated with fear and anxiety. Fear that is associated with any of the life domains, particularly within the family, can have a devastating effect on our identity and the extent to which we are able to recover from distress. If, however, we continually replenish our internal resources through daily prayer, meditation and faith it will support what is at the core of our being and it will reinforce our life purpose and give us a greater chance of rising out of the ashes or coming through the storm. The wheel of life is ever turning, each domain has its role to play so that when we are depleted in one area, we can draw from another life domain to positively build our strength. Resilience in each domain eventually builds character and leads to survival.

An important factor was how the women gained the will to become optimistic and hopeful in order to rise above their circumstances. The turning point arrived when the spirit of optimism took root, and eventually broke through the barren soil of despondency. It was a subtle shift akin to the first light at dawn after a long and dark night. Optimism became the substance for a transformation, foreshadowing a brighter chapter in their lives.

This study showed that it was the capacity to get up and go again which ultimately produced growth, particularly when it was augmented by seeking and undergirded by their belief system. Strength was based on inner resources, which in turn gave them the power to become resilient and to cope under severe conditions.

Motivation became a driving force, not only associated with personal determination but also by the communal support and love they received from family and friends. Faith and prayer weaved through the narratives, binding individuals together, giving them strength and the determination to survive. Beauty emerged not just from the individual understandings but from the collective utterances and the interwoven stories of triumph over adversity.

Epilogue

Challenges and Opportunities

Every challenge we face is the opportunity to become more than we have ever been.

UNKNOWN

Having completed this study of ten women, my thesis is that self-awareness is one of the keys that unlocks the door to resilience, thus promoting change and the ability to successfully recover from traumatic life events. While it may be difficult for some people to exercise faith as they are facing challenges, it is what becomes their saving grace. For those who believe and trust in a benevolent God and use the tool of prayer it leads them to find peace in the midst of the storm. Not everyone has a belief system, but those who profess a faith and have a strong belief system can with the help of God overcome, because it gives a strong connection with a positive force and one that is higher than them.

Mental health problems have a way of altering our thought processes and tricking us into thinking that the quest for beauty is impossible. Under intense pressure, it is difficult to see through the gloom and darkness. The feeling of being undeserving, worthless, hopeless and helpless diminishes one's ability to feel happy.

The ability to access different forms of support during a time of crisis is an important element in how people regain their coping capacity.

It is worth noting that there are different types of support we can call on during times of distress. Each will allow the beauty in ourselves and others to shine through the commitment to service. There is beauty in each type of support.

A) Familial support: this type of support combats distress and generally come from people who are closest to us and within our kinship network. It is a systemic approach to survival, in that the notion of each one helps one is activated.

B) Social support: This type of support augments familial support through services within a community. Resources are provided by professionals who assess and respond to need. Those who are unable to call on family members will find social support helpful in buffering stress.

C) Collegial support: comes from people within the work environment. Colleagues can become close by lending a helping hand and a listening ear. A person who is struggling is helped to recognise and build their confidence.

D) Financial Support: this type of support is a cross between family and social support. Both systems are based on either giving or lending money. Financial support has the purpose of helping those who are in need of practical support, but it can be the most difficult type of support to give and receive.

E) Spiritual support: This type of support comes from people who are connected by their values, faith, beliefs and prayer. It transcends all other types of support because it promotes overall wellness of mind, body and soul. It provides hope to stand against any foe and it allows the door to open to spiritual regeneration and true beauty.

When we are given words of encouragement it helps to lift the spirit and gives the belief that we can succeed. The study confirmed that going through an experience that is analogous with going through ashes or a storm can be life-threatening. Yet, with the right tools and the ability to trust God and develop hope in the midst of our troubles, it is possible to draw on one's inner strength. We can rise to a new beginning.

Relationships are at the heart of how we function as human beings, they are life sustaining. However, the reality is that relationships can bring joy and sorrow, they can make us feel happy or sad, they can bring gladness or despair. How we respond to the disappointments we face in any type of situation, is more often than not, a test of character.

The ability to forgive, and let go, sets us free from the past. The more we hold onto the wrongs that others have done to us, the more we subject ourselves to pain. While it is hard to forgive in some circumstances, we can also learn that forgiveness is not only for others but for us. Rising out of the ashes and coming through the storm is about how we respond to adversity. The more emotionally intelligent we become, the easier it will be to ask God to show us how to rise above our circumstances, that is inevitably how we navigate the quest for beauty.

With the challenges of life there are infinite opportunities to overcome and adapt to our circumstances. It is important to remember that it is not the past that defines us, but the future we are hoping to achieve. It is with patience and perseverance that we are able to overcome traumatic and life-threatening experiences and move along another path. It is the path to wellness and ultimately restoration.

The quest for beauty is infinitely complex against a backdrop of distress, physical, emotional and psychological pain. Nevertheless, the good news is that it is possible to find a way through it by trusting God to direct your path as well as through your individual efforts and the social support you are able to gain from others. The beauty shines through when we discover that whether we go through ashes or storm God is with us.

> Let the beauty of Jesus be seen in me
> All his wonderous compassion and purity
> Oh, thou Spirit divine,
> All my nature refine
> Till the beauty of Jesus be seen in me.

TOM M JONES

References

Armstrong, L. (1967). *A Wonderful World*.

Becker-Phelps, L. Kayle, M. (2016). *Love: The Psychology of Attraction*. Penguin Random House: London.

Bhagwandas, A. (2023). *Ugly: Giving Us Back Our Beauty Standards*. Blink Publishing: London.

Boom, C.T. with Elizabeth and John Sherrill. (1971). *The Hiding Place*. Chosen Books: Grand Rapids, Michigan.

Briscoe, C. (2007). *Beyond Ugly*. Hodder and Stoughton: London.

Brown, B. (2015). *Daring Greatly: How the Courage to be Vulnerable Transforms the Way We Live, Love, Parent and Lead*. Avery.

Cohler, B. (1987). *Adversity, Resilience, and the Study of Lives*, In E.J. Anthony & B. Cohler (Eds.). *The Invincible Child* (pp. 363–424). New York: Guildford.

DePrince, M & E. (2015). *Hope in a Ballet Shoe*. Faber & Faber: London.

De Gaulle. (1940). *The flames of French resistance must not and shall not die*. 18th June 1940 In Montefiore, S. (2005). Queens Publishing Limited: London.

Frank, A. (1947). *The Diary of a Young Girl*. Otto Frank.

Garvey, M. (1986) *The Life and Opinions of Marcus Garvey* (Vol.1), Amy Jacques Garvey (ed.) Majority Press. New York.

Gaither, G. (1971). *Something Beautiful, Something*. CCLI Number 18060.

Hoge, R. (2013). *Ugly*. Hachette: Australia.

Hume, D. (1757) *Of the Standard of Taste: Essays Moral and Political*. George Routledge and Sons. London.

Ince-Greenaway, L. (2021). *Hard Truth: Growing Out of Adversity*. The Choir Press: Gloucester.

Jeffers, S. (2007) *Feel the Fear and Do It Any Way: How to Turn Your Fear and Indecision into Confidence and Action*. Vermillion, London.

King, Martin Luther Jnr. (1963), *'I have a dream.'* March on Washington.

Kubler-Ross, E. (1970). *On Death and Dying.* Macmillan: New York.

Kushner, H. S. (1981). *When Bad Things Happen to Good People.* Anchor Books: New York.

Ledesma, J. (2014). *Conceptual Frameworks and Research Models on Resilience in Leadership.* Sage Open, 4(3), 1–8).

Luthar, S; Cicchetti, D; and Becker, B. (2000) *The Construct of Resilience: A Critical Evaluation and Guidelines for Future Work.* Child Development, 7 (3), 543–562

Mandela, N. (2005). *I am the first accused.* In Montefiore, S. *Speeches That Changed the World: The Stories and Transcripts of Moments That Made History.* Quercus Publishers.

McCubbin, H., Thompson, E., Thompson, A. and Futrell, A. (1999). *The Dynamics of Resilient Families* Sage Publications: London.

Maraboli, S. (2009). *Life the Truth and Being Free.* Better Today Publishing.

Masten, A., Best, K.M. and Garmezy, N. (1990). Resilience and Development; Contributions From the Study of Children Who Overcome Adversity. *Development and Psychopathology*, 2, 425–444.

Parker, S., Sachar Sidhu, N., Szudek, A., Uwannah, V., and Weeks, M. (2022). *Simply Psychology.* Penguin Random House: London.

Parks-Porterfield, M. (2007). *Treating Depression Naturally.* Teach Services Inc.: Brushton, New York.

Rath, T., and Clifton, D. (2004). *How Full is Your Bucket?* The Gallop Press: New Jersey.

Seligman, M. E. (1975). *Helplessness. On Depression, Development and Death.* W.H Freeman.

Southwick, S. M., Bonanno, G. A., Masten, A. S., Panter-Brick, C., & Yehuda, R. (2014). Resilience Definitions, Theory, and Challenges: Interdisciplinary Perspectives. *European Journal of Psychotraumatology*, 5(1), 25338.

Taylor, S. (2011). Social Support: A Review. In *The Oxford Handbook of Health and Psychology*. Oxford University Press: New York.

Tutu, D. & Tutu, M. (2014). *The Book of Forgiving: The Fourfold Path for Healing Ourselves and Our World*. Harper One: New York NY.

Vanzant, I. (1993). *Acts of Faith: Daily Meditations for People of Colour*. Simon & Schuster Inc.: United states of America.

Williams, D., Lawrence, A., Davis, B., and Vu, C. (2019) *Understanding How Discrimination Can Affect Health*. National Library of Medicine.

INTERNET SOURCES

American Psychological Association: https://advising.unc.edu/wp-content/uploads/sites/341/2020/07/The-Road-to-Resiliency.pdf

Carver, G.W. Brainy quotes https://www.goodreads.com/quotes/610935-99-of-failures-comes-from-those-who-have-a-habit

Crouch, A. Through it All. https://www.youtube.com/watch?v=xO5Qt2VQn4k

Department of Health https://www.nidirect.gov.uk/articles/recognising-adult-abuse-exploitation-and-neglect

Gandhi M. https://www.goodreads.com/author/quotes/5810891.Mahatma_Gandhi

Gould, L. https://www.goodreads.com/quotes/407329-sometimes-god-calms-the-storm-but-sometimes-god-lets-

Helen Keller: https://www.goodreads.com/quotes/3443-when-one-door-of-happiness-closes-another-opens-but-often

Jones, T. https://www.youtube.com/watch?v=yH9pNC67KZc

Mote, Edward 1985 https://eu.staugustine.com/story/lifestyle/faith/2015/09/10/story-behind-song-solid-rock/16264474007/

https://www.healthaffiliatesmaine.com/can-self-reflection-help-my-mental-health/Health encyclopedia

Nazim Hikmet https://www.blinkist.com/magazine/posts/10-beautiful-day-quotes-embrace-beauty-life

Neibuhr, R. https://www.lords-prayer-words.com/famous_prayers/god_grant_me_the_serenity.html

Newton, J https://hymnary.org/text/amazing_grace_how_sweet_the_sound

https://www.brainyquote.com/quotes/dale_carnegie_132157 Brainy Quotes

Odunayo, O. https://www.instagram.com/callmepod1/p/C_qapMvNypW/?hl=en&img_index=3

University of Rochester: Medical Centre https://www.urmc.rochester.edu/
encyclopedia/content.aspx?contenttypeid=1&contentid=4700#:~:text=P
eople%20who%20are%20socially%20connected,didn't%20feel%20as
%20depressed.

Roosevelt, F. https://historymatters.gmu.edu/d/5057/

Stevenson, M. https://thebottomofabottle.wordpress.com/2013/03/23/
footprints-in-the-sand-by-mary-stevenson/

World Health Organisation: https://scholar.google.co.uk/scholar?hl=en&as
_sdt=0%2C5&as_vis=1&q=world+health+organisation+definition+of+
health&btnG=

https://www.umc.org/en/content/how-faith-builds-your-resilience-skills

https://eu.staugustine.com/story/lifestyle/faith/2015/09/10/story-behind-
song-solid-rock/16264474007/

World Health Organisation: https://www.who.int/data/gho/data/major-
themes/health-and-well-being

Bible Text

Chapter Ten
Psalms 139:9-12
Philippians 4:6
1 Samuel 1 and 2
Hebrews 11:1

Chapter Eleven
Luke 5: 4-6
Matthew 13:31
Jonah Chapters 1-4
1 Corinthians 10:13
Luke 6:37

Chapter Twelve
Luke 11:9

Chapter Thirteen
John 3:16
Acts 17:28
Luke Chapter 17
Jerimiah 8:1-4
John 17:20-21

Chapter Fourteen
Romans 12:2
James 1:5-8
Micha 7:19
Luke 23:34
Proverbs 29:25
Isaiah 41:10
Isaiah 65:24
Isaiah 40:31
Hebrews 12:2
Psalms 139:14-16

www.ingramcontent.com/pod-product-compliance
Ingram Content Group UK Ltd.
Pitfield, Milton Keynes, MK11 3LW, UK
UKHW020704260325
456749UK00007B/865